Start & Run a
Computer Repair
Service

Start & Run a Computer Repair Service

Philip Spry and Lynn Spry

Self-Counsel Press
(a division of)
International Self-Counsel Press Ltd.
USA   Canada

Self-Counsel Press acknowledges the financial support of the Government of Canada through the Canada Book Fund (CBF) for our publishing activities.

Printed in Canada.

First edition: 2011

Library and Archives Canada Cataloguing in Publication

Spry, Lynn, 1974–
    Start & run a computer repair service / Lynn Spry and Philip Spry.

ISBN 978-1-77040-089-4

    1. Computer service industry — Management. 2. Computers — Maintenance and repair — Management. 3. New business enterprises — Management. I. Spry, Philip II. Title. III. Title: Start and run a computer repair service.

HD9696.67.A2S67 2011   338.4'7004   C2011-904545-1

MIX
Paper from
responsible sources
FSC® C004071

Self-Counsel Press
(a division of)
International Self-Counsel Press Ltd.

1704 North State Street   1481 Charlotte Road
Bellingham, WA 98225   North Vancouver, BC V7J 1H1
USA   Canada

Contents

Notice to Readers

Laws are constantly changing. Every effort is made to keep this publication as current as possible. However, the author, the publisher, and the vendor of this book make no representations or warranties regarding the outcome or the use to which the information in this book is put and are not assuming any liability for any claims, losses, or damages arising out of the use of this book. The reader should not rely on the author or the publisher of this book for any professional advice. Please be sure that you have the most recent edition.

Introduction

I love computers and have since I was in my early teens. Over the decades, I've watched them develop from giant clunky boxes with green screens to tiny works of art that project photo-realistic games on monitors the size of walls. I eagerly read each new issue of *Byte* and *PC Magazine*, waiting for the next breakthrough in hardware and software; it's probably fair to classify me as a computer enthusiast.

As a hobby, it's relatively inexpensive. Think about it — the most expensive desktop CPU in existence at any given time is usually a little more than $1,000. That's it! Imagine having the ability to buy a Formula 1 race car engine and pop it into your car for less than the cost of cable TV for a year! Of course, engines don't double in power every two years, but the ease and simplicity of computer upgrades have made most of us relative experts in working on our own systems.

Six years ago I was in this position. I had built my own computers for years and was the guy everyone came to for help. I'd been an IT professional for more than a decade so when my wife Lynn and I started looking for business opportunities we saw a computer store as a natural fit. I'd managed people for years and I loved computers. What could be better? I found a profitable store for sale, bought it, and prepared to enjoy my hobby while the money rolled in!

What followed were the most grueling three years of my life. My wife and I received a crash course in retail sales, customer service, follow-up, technical support, marketing, and on-site service. The lessons in this book are the direct result of years of trial and error, and of failing miserably and working through it, to emerge successful, happy, and profitable.

Books, Websites, and Other Resources

This book is focused on giving you the critical information you need to begin on the right foot, but as you grow you will run into situations where additional help is required. As much as we'd love to have a comprehensive collection of answers for every situation you might encounter, it's just not reasonable or even possible. Fortunately, we live in an age where information is only a few clicks away!

For instance, while we may recommend inexpensive sources of advertising that have been effective for us, there are entire books and websites dedicated to finding the most effective advertising for your business. Therefore, throughout this book, you will find links to websites, books, and resources that can help you find what's best for you.

That said, we cannot guarantee that the resources listed will be the best for you or your business. Sure, there are others out there and you may find better or worse, but these are the ones we have used successfully and believe have fair prices and good service. We don't get anything from these sites for mentioning them and they are listed here because they helped us and we hope they can help you.

Forms

Throughout this book, you will find many references to forms and other documents that you can use in your business. Each of these documents is on the CD included with this book. Before you use any of these documents, you should consult your own attorney or accountant as the laws in your state or province may be different and the documents may need to be worded differently to be applicable in your area.

Computer Repair: An Opportunity in Any Economy

Almost six years ago, my wife and I decided we were done being corporate drones and working 70 hours a week climbing the ladder of success. We'd chased the corner office, we'd taken endless flights, and we were tired of our shoulders drooping from carry-ons packed with multiple laptop computers. There was no end in sight and we realized it was time for a change. Fortunately, our timing couldn't have been better.

In 2006, the economy was booming and people had more money than they knew how to spend. The real estate market was going crazy and houses were appreciating at 30 percent per year. The instant equity created allowed people to take out loans — there was disposable cash everywhere! With this much cash in the economy, new construction and new businesses opened daily. Instead of clawing and scratching for every dollar, many business owners just hung out their shingles and waited for people to show up — and show up they did!

As suited corporate members, we were used to spending years working on projects only to see them abandoned when new leadership came in. We needed a change. We considered opening a consulting firm, but the market was flooded with them and we didn't know how we could differentiate ourselves. A friend of our suggested we look into purchasing a business instead of starting one from scratch. He said we might be able to save ourselves some time and money by plugging ourselves into a company with a proven revenue stream. It sounded good, but which company? There were thousands!

We began our research. If memory serves, we looked at more than 3,500 businesses in the Phoenix area alone! We checked out everything from coin-operated Laundromats to print shops. There were so many interesting opportunities and as we continued to research, we realized each of them was missing something. During a strong economy, they could make money, but if anything were to happen, they would be in real trouble. For example, selling high-end granite kitchen counters is fine when million-dollar homes are being built faster than people can buy them, but bull markets can't last forever and we were looking for something long-term. So, what type of business could grow during both economic growth and economic recession?

3

Just when we were about to give up, we found one business that looked really promising. It was a local computer store and it was selling computers as fast as the staff could build them! The store was packed with people, it was stocked from floor to ceiling, and the employees were happy. This business looked like many of the businesses we'd seen but one thing stood out — it didn't just sell a particular item, the staff did repairs as well! This, combined with my personal interest in computers made this business a very strong candidate.

When you run any business you can only sell two things: time and components. Computer businesses are no different. If people aren't buying computers, they better be buying service or you're out of business. Fortunately, the single greatest reason customers enter our stores is because their computers are malfunctioning. Sure, some customers come to our stores because they want to upgrade or just need a new computer, but let's be honest, more than 80 percent of the time something's wrong.

However, the solution to this problem is to repair it or replace it. When people have money, they don't want to mess with the old system. They shrug like it's nothing for them and pay $2,000 on a new system. Why should they bother fixing their old system? They are people of means and see no reason to trifle with a dusty old piece of junk. Flash forward a few years; the home equity line of credit has been drained, the real estate bubble has popped, and the dusty piece of junk that will cost $100 to repair starts looking good.

If you don't have the ability to tap into this type of need, and your only revenue stream is component sales, it is monumentally harder to stay afloat. You might need to adapt to the market conditions, but you can survive. Businesses that don't have that capability are dying all around us while we prosper and expand because we have a business that services people in both an up and a down economy.

1. The Computer Business during a Boom

Of course, if the economy is doing well, people have money to spend and a computer business can make high profits. People buy new, high-end gaming machines, companies want expensive high-capacity servers, and businesspeople start shopping for the best laptops available. If you are in business during this economy, you can find that custom computers can routinely make margins as high as 30 to 40 percent. This means that on a $2,000 gaming system, retailers can make as much as $800 on one sale! During a booming economy, the computer business will realize the following:

- Customers choose to replace instead of repair broken computers. Customers often don't feel like investing $150 into an old computer when a new computer is only $400. Plus, they'll often give you the old one if you transfer their information to the new computer.

- Customers may bring in older, working machines and request a full rebuild of the computer (replacing all the interior parts to upgrade the machine).

- Customers consider fast computers a "need" instead of a "want." Businesses want bigger, better computers and servers to make their employees "faster." Individuals want better machines to allow them to play games, edit videos, and, in general, have a faster, better experience.

2. The Computer Business during a Bust

When the economy is doing poorly, people cut back. They start looking at ways to save money and repairing computers is often far less expensive than buying new machines. This means that while other businesses are watching their customers dwindle, sales plummet, and foot traffic reduce, a computer repair business actually starts to grow! This is what the business looks like during an economic recession:

- Customers choose repairs before replacement computers. If the customers feel they can spend $150 and get their computer running "like new," that is worthwhile compared to spending $400 or more to buy a new computer.

- Customers choose to upgrade one or two parts on an old machine. Sometimes these modifications (e.g., additional RAM, bigger hard drive) are less than $100 and will make the old computer as good as new for the customer.

- Customers buy lower-end refurbished systems. When people are looking to save money, refurbished computers fly off the shelves while the new ones gather dust.

3. A Business That Grows in Any Economy

Computer businesses that typically repair systems as well as sell computers can survive in booming or busted economies. Because we own a business that can grow in any economy, while most businesses were feeling the pressure, we were expanding. We opened a second location and later that year also began giving back through our Computers for Soldiers program. Not bad for a business during a recession!

What's even better about the computer business is that it has the opportunity to expand and grow depending on the services you offer. If you start getting business clients, you can grow your business to include maintenance plans and eventually handle the IT needs of businesses all over your area. Or, if you enjoy rebuilding machines, you can get into refurbished systems and sell online, in a retail store, or even become a wholesaler or recycler. In the computer business, there are so many ways to expand and grow that it is all up to you how you go about it!

 If you want some personal guidance before you jump in, you may want to contact SCORE — Counselors to America's Small Business! This group specializes in helping small businesses get off the ground, grow, and handle challenges. It is a great place to get some *free* advice and find lots of useful ideas and assistance. (www.score.org)

4. How Much Can You Make?

Your revenue depends on many things, including, but not limited to, number of hours worked, location, skill set, services offered, competition, and name recognition. Let's look at some examples.

4.1 Part time: Owner-only business

You've probably seen a part-time/owner-only business on Craigslist or other online classified ad websites. The owner may work a full-time job and do a small amount of computer work on the side. There is no dedicated phone line for the business but even if there is, only one person answers it. This is the most common of the part-time computer businesses and it can be a very nice source of additional income.

This type of business has a few regular customers and they all are serviced by the owner. There are no full-time employees and this one-person shop can handle 10 to 20 customers a week with most of them on the weekend. The rate these types of owners charge is usually less than a full-time operation, but they can still make $30 to $40 an hour! If they can up sell a few pieces of hardware, they can make $600 to $800 a week! For a part-time gig, that's pretty good money, but they are tied to their customers and can never get a break.

4.2 Full time: Owner-only business

If the business owner is a dedicated full-time employee, he or she will be able to take on many more customers. In general, it would be possible to have as many as three or even four on-site customers in one day — especially if some of the work is completed either remotely or at his or her business (or home) location. Add that to the other work brought back to the house or place of business and he or she can make a very nice living!

If you can multitask, you can do well in this kind of setup. For example, if you're the only one working, you get up in the morning, start the virus removals going, maybe start updating a few PCs, then head out. You work as quickly as possible, get a few customers taken care of, and then head back to your base of operation. Run more antivirus tools, maybe start a wipe and reload, then head back out. Take care of a few more customers, bring back the PCs

that are too difficult to deal with and work on them. If you do this and build a solid list of clients, you can do very well, but you will work seven days a week.

When you're the only person in your business, people think of you as their computer person. You're not a firm with whom they deal, but you're the person on whom they rely and if you can't help them out, they take it personally. It's important to set boundaries and let people know from the start when you're available. Stick to that and set pricing accordingly. Never underestimate how much your time is worth. In this business model, you're the linchpin for many companies and time given to one person can be time stolen from another.

4.3 Full time: Business has employees

Once a business expands to be big enough to employ others, your income is only restrained by the opportunity for work. A business owner can add employees as the work grows and will be increasing his or her income with each new employee! As long as the owner is careful to only add employees when they are required the business can continue to grow. The problem some owners have is that employees will always complain they have too much work to do and that there are never enough people. We were caught in this trap early on and we hired too many people. Funny thing was the work didn't get out the door faster. Turned out, we had the wrong people, not too few people!

It is absolutely critical that every single person you employ pays for himself or herself. You can *never* hire someone who is just nice to have around. If the employee doesn't do the tasks that earn the amount of money you pay him or her, get rid of the person.

As you grow, you can leverage your employees to take on larger and more complex projects and, remember, the more employees you have, the more money you are able to make. As long as you keep your costs low, you can keep on growing! Once you start growing there is no limit on the income that can be earned through the computer business. You can franchise your business model or even sell it entirely! Once you start one business, you'll become addicted to starting more.

5. Are You Qualified?

First, you need to know what your role will be. Do you want to manage a team of technicians and handle the financial end of the business while leaving the day-to-day servicing of computers to your employees? That's a good goal to pursue, but if you're just starting out, that's probably not the case.

Let's focus on someone who wants to do the work initially and then branch out as he or she grows. With this in mind, what qualifies someone to repair computers? Unlike some industries that have rigid certification requirements, there are no rules for becoming a great computer technician. Over the years, I have hired (and fired) many technicians. I have found great technicians who were teenagers that only started working on computers a few years earlier as well as experienced veterans with decades of time in the field. I have also seen people who have worked as computer techs for years (usually at some big-box stores) that couldn't pass our initial screening exam. So, what does it take to be a great computer repair technician?

- **Patience:** First and foremost you must be patient. Not all computer problems are solved quickly and not all customers are wonderful. However, if you have patience, you can get through just about anything.

- **Problem-solving skills:** About 95 percent of the problems you will see are the same (e.g., if the hard drive clicks, well, the hard drive is probably bad). However, 5 percent of the time, it's something that's not obvious and you need to be able to figure out what the issue is. That means troubleshooting, swapping components, trying different solutions, and persevering until you figure out what's wrong.

- **Positive attitude:** People will forgive a lot *if* you have a good attitude so be upbeat, happy, and positive. When you run into a problem, as frequently happens, make sure you give the customer solutions, not facts. Telling a customer that viruses have destroyed the Master Boot Record is just giving them information. Instead, tell the customer that while the virus screwed up his or her software, you have the tools to recover the data but it will take some time. The better your attitude, the better your customer's attitude! You drive his or her perceptions. If the customer sees you as angry and irritated, he or she will react accordingly.

- **Love of computers:** If you don't love them, you will hate them. Maybe not at first, but eventually. Computer repair is about problem solving, research, and results. The tough part is the repetition. Sure, you'll get a fun problem where the computer randomly shuts off although all the hardware tests perfect and it only happens after 9:00 p.m., but this is the exception to the rule. Most of the time you'll get machines with bad hard drives, bad power supplies, or ones riddled with viruses. Those three problems comprise the vast majority of the problems you'll encounter so you better get used to fixing them. With that said, you'll learn something new every single day. You can't help it. There are too many ways for computers to get screwed up and a seemingly infinite number of people to break them. So when you're working on the easy ones, let your brain focus on the tough ones. That leads nicely into the next point — multitasking.

• **Multitasking:** The most profitable technicians are the ones that can work on more than one system at a time. This is because many repairs require scans that will take hours; software installations that can take 15 to 20 minutes and downloads that can take hours, depending on the speed at which you're downloading. While the computer is working on that task, you want to shift and work on another. A common problem we run into is Windows shutting down unexpectedly or even briefly displaying the Blue Screen of Death (BSOD). While there are many reasons this can happen, a common cause is a failing hard drive. To test for this, we boot the computer into a special disk that automatically tests the entire system, including the hard drive. This can take anywhere from 15 minutes to several hours. Can you imagine if you only worked on one computer at a time? You'd sit there staring at the computer and nothing would be accomplished. Instead, move to the next computer, diagnose a third, start scans on a fourth, and get as much work out the door as possible. Time is money and you *must* use your time wisely.

• **Experience:** Yes, this is last, mainly because experience will be gained. The more you work on computers, the more you will learn. My wife actually worked in our stores for a few months. Although she wasn't a big fan of hardware repairs (her background was programming) after a month or so, she was completing hardware and software repairs for customers. Experience can be gained quickly and easily, but it takes concentration and determination. There are untold numbers of books on how to fix a computer. For that matter, following a simple troubleshooting chart can take you through most of the problems you'll see. There's a good example of a Boot Failure Troubleshooting Flowchart you can follow at www.fonerbooks.com/poster.pdf. The more computers you repair and the more accustomed you become to them, the more confident you'll be and the faster you'll solve problems. It has come to the point where I have solved a problem without even seeing a computer. When a customer walks in and says that his or her computer doesn't turn on even when he or she presses the button, my first instinct is that the power supply has died. It's common to see many dead power supplies in places where the power fluctuates. While it may seem like magic to know what's wrong with a PC before I even start to diagnose it, it's just because I've seen it so many times before. The same will happen to you and you'll be seen as a wizard!

If you think that these points describe you, then you may be on your way to owning a successful computer business!

6. Why You Don't "Need" Technology Certifications

For the purpose of actually fixing computers, certifications provide very little value. You can teach someone to troubleshoot a computer and in a few weeks he or she will be amazing, but he or she can have all the certifications in the world and not know how to open a computer case. There are some certifications that are commonly required to work at many of the big-box stores but I've interviewed hundreds of people with those qualifications and they rarely display any actual knowledge.

The exception to the rule is certifications from Microsoft: They still don't replace experience but they indicate a degree of knowledge that can be useful when determining whether to hire one candidate over another.

Honestly, a certification is mostly just for show. Despite the buzz value placed on them by some, they're generally only good when you're doing advertising. "All our technicians are ABC Certified so you *know* you can trust us!" So are we to believe that someone with ten years of experience and no certification is less valuable than someone with a nice piece of paper?

Certifications are nice to have and they show someone was interested enough in working on computers to get them, but that's probably it. We have seen plenty of certified technicians that are not half as competent as self-taught technicians. The difference is always experience. Sure, wiping a computer and reloading the operating system is easy 95 percent of the time. However, it is that 5 percent of the time where the operating system doesn't load, the updates won't run, or the drivers can't be found that makes the difference between a qualified technician and a

"certified idiot." With that said, if you employ people who do have certifications, by all means, display the certificates everywhere you can.

7. There Are Easy Ways to Solve New Problems

No matter how many years of IT experience you have, there will be problems you have never faced before. New products and services appear daily and it just isn't possible to keep current with all of them. With these new products come new problems. Solving them quickly and profitably is what being a computer tech is about. Don't forget, the longer a problem takes to solve, the less you earn to solve it. In a perfect world, every problem could be solved in less than a minute but that's just not the way it works.

Those of us who have been doing computer repair for years know there is nothing better than Google to troubleshoot an issue. Is there a random beep code? Google it. Does the customer have a virus you haven't seen before? Chances are someone else has already solved it. Whatever the problem, don't be afraid to leverage Google to find the answer. Chat rooms and discussion forums are full of technical problems and solutions. Fortunately for us, Google makes it easy to navigate the Web. Just type in the error code, computer type, or whatever makes the issue unique and you are bound to get tons of results.

I'm lazy. I fully accept that about myself. In my mind, why should I spend hours trying to figure out why something is broken when people much smarter than I am who have many more years of experience than I do have already solved it? It just doesn't make sense, but we have had technicians in the past too embarrassed to admit that they didn't know the answer to a problem. They have this idea that they are tech gods and all should defer to them, so when something happens they can't explain it drives them crazy. They will waste *hours* trying to figure out how to solve the problem instead of doing a simple search. The result: They are slow and inaccurate. I don't pay them to waste my money; I pay them to solve problems. That means as expeditiously as possible.

Get on the Internet and type in a few search terms. Odds are good that no matter what it is, someone else has faced it before and mentioned it on the Internet. Spending 30 minutes reading the forums and searching the Internet can replace days of frustration and lost revenue.

8. Getting Paid to Practice

Sure, you have fixed your computer and your friends' computers. Maybe you even helped people at work. However, that may seem different from working on a system that is owned by a complete stranger. If you want some extra practice before you jump into starting your own repair business, there are many ways that don't involve taking on your first actual paying customer. If you start by doing a paid on-site job, you're probably working while the customer is breathing down your neck asking you to explain everything you're doing. This adds more pressure than you need to your very first job, so how about getting some practice first?

One of the best ways to practice before you start your business is to work on used systems. This is a great way to get started for a couple of reasons:

- Used computers usually don't work or don't work well. After running computer repair stores for years, I can tell you this is very similar to what your customers will bring in. First, you don't know if they work; second, if they do work, you have no idea what is wrong.

- After you repair them, you can sell them as refurbished computers and you will be able to get paid for your practice!

There are a few good places to look for used computers. Usually, you can find low-cost machines at places like Goodwill and other charitable organizations. Another option is to look on Craigslist for computers that may not be in working condition. To get experience on desktop repairs, look for machines that meet the following standards:

- Certificate of Authenticity (COA), also known as the Operating System Key. Microsoft requires that every computer that runs their software is properly licensed. To that end, each system has a COA on it, stuck to the side, the back, the top, or the bottom. It's a white and greenish sticker with a bunch of six-digit alphanumeric groups. That key is used to reinstall the operating system. If you don't have this, you'll need to buy one if you're going to remain in compliance. Try to find computers that have Microsoft XP or newer operating systems (OS). Any OS before this will not be supported by Microsoft and is hard to work on anyway.

- Getting used RAM is almost as expensive as buying new RAM, so try to find a computer that already includes at least the minimum amount of RAM recommended for its OS. For example, if the computer has XP, make sure it has 512MB RAM. Any less and it will be so slow that you will become frustrated working on it. The good news is that even a computer in bad condition tends to have working RAM so this is one part that is usually recoverable on a used computer.

- The motherboard has *no* blown or leaking capacitors (caps); this is critical. Replacing a motherboard is expensive and if the motherboard has blown or leaking caps, it will need to be replaced. Some computers will work if the motherboard has capacitor problems, but it won't work well and it won't work for long. Since this is something that can be identified with a simple visual inspection, it is an easy way to avoid a problem.

- Unfortunately, there will be no easy way to tell if the CPU is working without powering up the computer. The good news is that CPUs are one of the least likely components to break. Therefore, if it is in the computer, there is a good chance that it works; however, if it is missing, getting a new CPU can be annoying and expensive. If the computer does not come with a CPU, you may as well look for another machine.

- In general, the case size doesn't matter from your perspective, but if it is a "slimline" computer, you should be aware that replacement parts (e.g., power supplies) are often built specifically for that machine. Custom power supplies are a fortune to replace. While a replacement power supply on your average computer can cost you about $20 from a wholesaler (less if it is used), a replacement for a slimline computer is almost always used and often runs around $100!

- In general, once a computer is refurbished, customers will judge its condition by its case. Even if you replace the entire inside of the computer with new components, a beat up case will make your customers wonder about the quality of the computer. The better the case, the easier it will sell.

- The CD/DVD drive component is not as critical. In general, most computers come with either a CD or DVD drive. If the one in the used computer doesn't work, you can probably get a used replacement for around $10 to $15.

- Even after you take all these precautions, odds are good that some computers you find will not be cost effective to repair. However, if you got them for a low enough price (i.e., less than $40), the experience you gain (and the parts you strip) should more than cover your cost.

If you are looking to learn more about laptop repair, try to restrict yourself at first to one type of laptop. Don't try to buy an HP, and then a Dell, and then an IBM. Instead, find one type of machine and try to find used computers of that type. Trying to fix a machine by replacing a screen is expensive if you need to order new parts to make the repair. However, it becomes more cost effective if you can take the screen from a machine with a bad motherboard and replace it on an otherwise working computer. So, maybe you can find a lot of IBM Think-Pads and just complete repairs on those systems. This will allow you to practice with one model and use the parts from the nonworking computers to fix the laptops that are close to working condition. Otherwise, if you try to practice on multiple brands and models, you will find that most laptop parts are not compatible with other models (except for RAM and hard drives) and you will wind up spending a great deal on replacement parts.

You will also find that buying used laptops, even in nonworking condition, is much more expensive than buying used working desktops. This is because the working parts of nonworking laptops are still expensive. For instance, a used laptop screen can retail for $80 or more! The good news is that the market for used laptops is always strong, so once the computer is up and running you should easily make back your money.

9. Working at Home versus Retail Storefront

Although we began our business through a retail storefront, you don't have to take the same path we did. It may be possible to immediately open a retail store but it might be prudent to start slowly.

You can have a thriving business working out of your home using the exact same marketing and advertising strategies we use in the retail space. You can create a wide customer base and become profitable much more quickly working from home rather than if you had to recoup the start-up costs of a retail storefront. You can sell parts, repair computers, and even build custom systems from your home. Your growth potential is limited working from home but your start-up costs are so low it's a very safe way to dip your toes into the waters of computer service.

Table 1 outlines some things to consider when deciding between working from home and opening a retail storefront.

9.1 Finding a location for a retail storefront

The answer to where to locate your business is extremely simple in this day and age. Everyone uses computers so you can have a successful business almost anywhere! Some places are better than others, but no matter where you go, it's possible to create a successful business model that is flexible enough to take advantage of the local demographics. Your fundamental goal is to provide a service that the local population can't easily replicate. Let's take a look at Table 2.

Table 2 shows just a few examples but you can see how tailoring your services to the demographics of the area can help you become successful in any environment. The only requirement is that there are people who have computers. Everything else is up to you!

One common issue people raise is the presence of some of the larger computer stores in a given neighborhood. Don't let that stop you. No matter what other businesses are in your area, large or small, there are still opportunities for a profitable computer repair business. For instance, one of our stores is right around the corner from one of the "big-box" computer stores. The store has tens of thousands of square feet of floor space, hundreds of associates, and nearly any component you can imagine for sale, often with multiple alternatives. No point in trying to compete, right? Wrong!

Big-box stores are very different from smaller, more agile shops. There are huge differences

TABLE 1
WORKING FROM HOME VERSUS RETAIL STOREFRONT

	Home	Retail Storefront
Cost	**Very Low** If you are growing your business from your home, typically you will not have very high set-up costs. As a matter of fact, the space and utilities you use for your business can actually be tax deductible, thus reducing your personal expenses!	**High** If you are looking to open a retail location, there are many expenses that you will need to pay. Costs will include rental agreements (e.g., first month's rent, security deposit), utilities, signage, full inventory, and more. Be prepared to spend anywhere from $20,000 or more on even the most conservative retail location.
Speed to Opening	**Immediate** If you choose to run a business from your home, you can get started almost immediately. There is very little lead time and you can be in business as soon as you get your initial set-up items completed.	**3 to 6 Months** Retail stores tend to take three to six months to start up *after* a location is identified. The lease has to be negotiated, the contract has to be signed, and the store has to be set up. When we started our second store this took only a few months, but some business owners spend as much as six months getting this started.
Management	**Easier** You already manage your home so running a business from home doesn't change anything (except for the work space you set aside)!	**Harder** Once you commit to a retail location, you will find that you have more to manage (e.g., rent, security).
Obtaining Customers	**Harder** Because you do not have a retail location you will not be able to benefit from customers driving by and seeing your new storefront. As a result, you will have to rely entirely on your marketing and advertising to bring in new customers.	**Easier** When you obtain a retail location, one of the things you are buying is the customer traffic that the location generates. Each day, a good location should give your business the ability to advertise to thousands of potential new customers.

TABLE 1 — CONTINUED

Customer Visits	**Limited** If you intend to run a business from your home, you may need to review your homeowner's association policy or insurance. It is possible that either (or sometimes both) will not permit customers on your property.	**Unlimited** If you have a retail storefront, you are allowed to use the space (generally) for any commercial purpose. This means that you can have business meetings, etc., at your location.
Credibility	**Lower** Unfortunately, working from home is sometimes a concern for customers. Because you don't have a retail location, some people will be concerned that you won't be in business for long. You will need to pay special attention to building credibility (see Chapter 3).	**Higher** Although many businesses fail each year, customers do see a business that has a retail location as being more of a "real" company. They are likely to assume that the business is more capable than one in a mobile location.
Ability to Grow	**Limited** In general, you will have less ability to grow your business from your home. For example, it will be more difficult to add new employees, or have customers visit your location. If your business grows beyond what you can handle, you may need to consider retail or commercial space.	**Infinite** Once you start running a retail location, you can grow your business to add other stores, or simply expand to additional office space. Many computer repair businesses have grown in this way (e.g., Data Doctors).

between the large, impersonal store and the close and personal service of a small store. Instead of the larger store hurting our sales, we found that many of our customers find us as they are driving to that "other" business! They know that the prices at large box stores are often very high for computer repair and they may decide to try a local business instead. Imagine that; we get customers *because* there is a big-box store in the area that does computer repair. Also, many customers like the idea of dealing with the same person all the time. That's

unrealistic to expect in a store that employs a hundred or more people, so in our smaller store our customers get the value of familiarity.

Another thing that people often worry about is that a large retailer will take all the computer sales from the business. What we have found is that this is not the case at all. We actually have a business in a Walmart shopping center. While there is the risk of losing business to a large store such as Walmart, we still find bargain hunters that buy our products instead

TABLE 2
WHERE TO LOCATE A RETAIL STOREFRONT

Demographics	Need	Service and Products
Businesses	Maintenance and reliability	Service contracts, servers, regular visits, and printers
Younger (college students, etc.)	Newest technology	High-end, flashy systems and multimedia PCs.
Older	Simplicity and reliability	Classes, patience, and inexpensive computers
Families	Safety, homework, and home entertainment systems	Internet security, educational systems and software, and reporting software

of theirs. Being a small repair shop, we have the opportunity to tune our offerings to compliment the large behemoth (e.g., we don't compete on new laptop prices with Walmart). While Walmart does sell computers, they don't build custom systems with high-end parts. As a result, Walmart employees have actually been known to send *us* business!

In other places, there may be no other store or competition, but that doesn't mean that people don't need computer repair — just the opposite. In some areas, a lack of businesses may mean a golden opportunity to fill a real need in your community; in this case, there is even less need to start a retail store at first. If there is no competition, it means that people are either living with problem computers or they are driving dozens of miles just to get to a repair store! You may find that your store will grow quickly just from word of mouth!

Wherever you are, one of the best parts of being in the computer business is that it is a business that can exist in any town, in any part of any country. With the low entry costs and

high immediate return, it is easy to test an area before you commit!

If you have experience running a retail store or have significant capital, starting with a storefront may be the way to go. We only recommend this if you have significant financial resources and are sure this business is for you. It may be months until you're profitable and you don't want to put all of your money into a venture, sign multiyear leases, hire employees, buy equipment, get everything set up, and then realize you don't actually want to do this as a profession.

9.2 Working from home

One of the best parts of getting into computer repair is that you can ease into it. You don't need a special permit, expensive equipment, or even a special license. It's just you and your own hard work!

The best advantage to starting this type of business is that you can test the waters by starting part time and increasing your hours as your business becomes profitable. It's tempting to jump right in and open a store, but if you haven't done anything like this before, take our advice and tread with care. You may have a strong idea you eventually want to open a store, but if you want to save a few dollars and start slowly, the easiest way to get started is to begin as a part-time, home-based company. This will let you invest the available time you have for the lowest amount of money. As the business grows, you can decide how to expand.

If you are currently employed, starting a computer repair business is an easy way to supplement your income. Before you start running ads, decide when you will be available. If you have a day job, you may want to focus on finding customers who need "after hours" service. This will let you charge a premium for your service while building your customer base. It's important to decide this in the beginning. A critical part of creating satisfied customers is meeting expectations. If you know your boss has called a meeting for 9:00 a.m. the next day you can't expect to work until 2:00 a.m. on the side as your primary job will suffer. With this in mind, create a time range in which you're comfortable working and stick to it. Customers will naturally push you to work outside of your time frame, but if you stick to the stated times, they will respect your boundaries. You must be consistent. If you arrive late or don't have the expected work done on time, customers will expect you to make up that time elsewhere.

10. How Much Will It Cost to Start Your Business?

One of the first questions you may consider is how much it will cost to start your own computer repair business. The short answer is that it depends on what you want to do. One of the best parts about starting a computer repair business is that the start-up costs are dramatically less than they are for other businesses. If you want to open a restaurant, you'll need ovens, sinks, disposal, venting, a theme, tables, chairs, glasses, dishwashers, a full staff, and menus — it's easy to spend $150,000 getting it ready.

As a point of contrast, when we opened our second retail store we spent less than $30,000. That sounds like quite a bit, but consider that included the entire interior setup, all the inventory, the signs, the computers to run the place, the software, the lease, the security deposit, as well as the phone system and all the tools. In addition, we became profitable in our second month of operation without any advertising whatsoever. I'm not suggesting you go this route; it's a decision not to be made lightly, but knowing how much less it is to build a turnkey operation can help you make that call.

If you choose to forgo a retail location and simply work from your home, the start-up costs are almost nonexistent and you can

Rich Dad's Before You Quit Your Job: Ten real-life lessons every entrepreneur should know about building a multimillion-dollar business, by Robert T. Kiyosaki with Sharon L. Lechter: This was the first book we read about owning a small business and the information in it was very helpful. The discussion isn't just about opening a business, but also why you should and what it will entail. This book covers the risks and rewards that come from leaving a permanent position and pursuing business entrepreneurship.

easily get started for less than $1,000. The biggest reason for this is that you probably already have most of the things you need.

The following are some of the things you will need to get started:

- **Website:** Do you need a website on your first day? Of course not. With that said, many people use the Internet to find low-cost computer repair so there's no reason to neglect this form of advertising. Purchase a name that's easy to remember, get it hosted through one of the many hosting services and you'll be well on your way! A single page with your services and telephone number will do to start. You don't need a full e-commerce site to get a customer. Every time you're thinking of spending money, ask yourself this question: "When will this purchase pay for itself?" When you're just starting, especially if you're working from your home, if you can't answer "immediately," don't spend the money. (See Chapter 3 for more information about building your website.)

- **Contact number:** You should have a dedicated business phone line. However, a cell phone can be a great way to dedicate a line without breaking the bank — initial cost between $0 (if you already have a cell phone you can use) to $100 per month. A nice way to have a dedicated line without spending any money is to use Google Voice. They will give you a number that's 100 percent free and will forward calls to your cell phone when you want them to. That way, you will have a separate line but can choose to answer it or not.

- **Equipment:** In general, you will need some equipment to get started but it doesn't have to be expensive. The only pieces of hardware you'll absolutely need are a power supply tester and a screwdriver. It's helpful to have an external hard drive, a flash drive, an external floppy drive (yes, sometimes they're needed), extra sticks of RAM, etc., but you can get started with less. You will need software, but there are so many free applications available that there's no reason to spend money on the corporate versions until you've exhausted the usefulness of the free ones. (See Chapter 5 for more information about tools of the trade.)

If you try, you can keep your costs low and your profits high. Just make sure that every item you purchase is *needed* and not just *wanted*.

> Not sure where to start? In the US, the Small Business Administration (SBA) has a lot of great resources for the small-business owner — and it's all *free*! You can find links to everything your small business needs including ideas to reduce tax burdens, ways to get grants and loans, instructions on finding business licenses, and much more! (See www.sba.gov.)

2

Starting
Your
Business

Once you decide that a computer repair business is right for you, it's time to start your business!

1. Create a Business Plan

One of the most valuable things you can do to start your business is to create a business plan. This is considered a living document that you can use to consolidate your current ideas and future plans for your business. A good business plan will include everything from how your business will be financed to how it will grow and expand. It is basically a repository of all that your business "plans" to do.

First and foremost, realize that a business plan is a living (or working) document and it should be created to fit your personality as well as your business. There is no one answer to what should go into a business plan. Some business plans are hundreds of pages long and include extensive information about the business owners, their financial situation, the plans for the business, five-year plans, etc. If you plan to obtain a financial investment, this is the type of document you will need. Investors (e.g., financial institutions and venture capitalists) will want all the information they can get and your business plan is the document in which they expect to find it all. However, if you are creating a business plan that represents a small home-based business, your document will be considerably shorter. There is no need to add tax returns to a document only you will be reading.

In general, do not expect a business plan to take one day or even one week! A business plan is simply a repository of all that you learn as you "plan" to open your business. Therefore, while you may complete a rough draft in one afternoon, as you start making decisions about your business, you should continue to update the document. For instance, did you take the weekend and visit local computer stores to learn about how they do business? If so, take what you learned and update the "competition" section of your business plan. Have you found a great online place to advertise? Write about it in your "marketing" section. Are you thinking about your five-year plan to franchise? Don't just keep it in your head, get it down on paper! Every day that you are thinking about or planning for your business is another day you will learn more about what your business will become.

Use your plan to capture all of your great ideas and plans in one place!

Before you begin creating your business plan, here are some tips that everyone should follow:

- **The length of the document is never as important as the content:** Make sure your plan is clear and concise, but has the detail you need to show your ideas will work.

- **Remember that your business plan is a living document:** Do not expect it to be "done" — ever. Plan to update this document regularly — even after you open your business. In the first year or two you may update it every six months. Moving forward, you may update it only once a year, but remember, it will need to be kept current.

- **Be specific:** Your plan is supposed to help you address the problems your business will encounter with specific, well-thought-out answers. If you aren't sure what the right answer is, research it until you are comfortable; don't just skip the section or problem.

- **Get feedback:** If you have partners, accountants, or family who are interested in the business, get their feedback on what you wrote. Make sure that they see your plan as realistic and not overly optimistic or pessimistic.

The following sections give a summary of the important parts of a business plan.

1.1 Executive summary

Every business plan, no matter the size of the company, should have a solid summary. In general, the summary should be short and to the point and at the very beginning of the document. It should give an overview of your company, and your long-term goals; however, it should not be more than a few paragraphs. Remember, if you are looking for investors, this will be the first thing that they read. A good executive summary will be interesting, show profit potential, and make the reader want to learn more about your business as an investment opportunity.

Although this is a summary of your business and the first section of your business plan, don't try to create this section first. Instead, you should plan to write this section last. The reason is that this section is basically a summary of the whole business plan which outlines your current situation and your future plans. Until you have a thoroughly created plan, you won't be prepared to create this section. Skip it for now and return to it after you have completed your full business plan.

1.2 Business description and vision

In this section you describe what your business is about, how it fits in the marketplace, how you will advertise it, and how you will operate. In general, as you start gathering information about your competition, figuring out your target market, etc., you can start entering the information into this area. The following

 Online Business Plan Template: One great resource for creating a useful business plan is the US Small Business Association (www.sba.gov). This site has everything you need to create a useful, clear, and concise business plan. They even offer an online form that helps you walk through your business plan creation.

points cover the sections to include in this part of your business plan:

- **Mission statement:** This section is usually a short sentence or two that summarizes the purpose of your business. Typically this mission will be shared with all of your customers, clients and employees, and be plastered on your websites, hung up in your store, etc.

- **Business vision:** This is the long-term vision for your business — or a statement of growth. It should include what your business wants to become and how you intend to get there.

- **Business product and services:** This area will allow you to describe what your business will do, how it fits in the marketplace and how it will make money. Outline all of your services and the products your business would like to carry. If you have any product flyers or detailed brochures, you can add them to your supporting documents.

- **Marketing and sales strategy:** Outline your plan for advertising, marketing, and networking. Include your costs, and your reasoning for choosing different venues.

- **Competition:** This section may be one of the most important. It should include descriptions of your strongest competitors, their locations (compared to yours), their specialties, and how you will compete against them. Also, consider what will make your business different from your competition.

- **Operating procedures:** Include how your business will run. It should include

everything from how your business will be organized, managed, and structured.

- **Business insurance and licenses:** This section should document what your business will need to operate. Include all documents in the supporting documents section (see section **1.4** for more information).

1.3 Financial data

One of the more exciting sections of your business plan is the financial documentation. These documents show how much your business expects to make and what the return on your investment will be. Unfortunately, this is also the section which will get the most scrutiny from investors. After all, your profitability will be based on assumptions and your investors will want to know just how you made these assumptions. It is one thing to say you can make $10,000 a month; it is another to prove it.

The best part about completing the financial section of your business plan is the confidence you will have about your business once you are done. Providing enough detail in this area will mean that there are few questions from investors.

The following sections should be included in the financial data section:

- **Start-up costs:** This includes all equipment, supplies, bills, and so forth to get your business off the ground.

- **Break-even analysis:** This area of the document describes when you think the business will "break even" or make its money back.

- **Profit and loss statement:** Every business should regularly generate a report like this as it shows how much your business made or lost on a regular basis. While the one you initially put in your business plan will be an estimate, you should update it regularly to represent your real values as your business grows.

- **Detailed monthly financial plan** (first year only): A detailed plan will show all of your monthly expenses and income for your first year of business. Be as detailed as possible. This section is invaluable as a planning tool. Every time you learn about a new expense or potential revenue, add something to this section. Make sure to add a corresponding note to your assumptions section.[1]

- **Detailed quarterly financial plan** (years two and three): Showing how your business should grow in the coming years lets you measure your progress as you go. Remember to keep your assumptions realistic.

- **Three-year expected summary:** This will show your three-year financial plan. While you may just break even or make a small amount of money in the first year, subsequent years should show a profit or your model may not be sound (make sure to add any necessary notes to the assumptions section).

One thing to check is that your assumptions are based on data instead of hope. Always double check all of your numbers to make sure that your assumptions are accurate and represent realistic sales and expenses. If you aren't sure, and think that a "range" would be more accurate, create your financials using a "worst case" and "best case" set of assumptions. Although this may not be included in most formal business plans, as a business owner, I know that showing your financials like this will give you a great baseline for your business. The "worst case" will help to prepare you for a slower than expected start and the "best case" will help you prepare for unexpected growth!

1.4 Supporting documents

The supporting documents section of the business plan is used to provide documents that your bank and investors will require. If you plan on launching a home-based business that will not have investors, you can generally skip this section. However, if you want to be prepared for when your business grows and you would like to get an investor, you may want to complete it now.

Each of the following documents is provided to prove that you are a solid investment and that your financial management is solid:

- **Tax returns of the business owner for the last two to three years:** Many banks will only require two years of tax returns, but having three available means that you will be prepared if they request the additional information.

- **Personal financial statements of the business owners:** The financial statements show where your money comes

---

[1] **Assumptions:** As you wrote up your financials, you made many assumptions. Since many of these assumptions apply to more than one area of the business plan, having a section with all your assumptions is a good way to consolidate your ideas. Make sure to list the details behind your reasoning and expectations. The more detail you have the more confident you will be in your financials.

from and where it goes. Typically, statements like these will include all of your assets and liabilities. Your bank can help you prepare these statements and will typically have forms that you can use.

- **Franchise documents:** If you are opening a computer repair franchise, you will need to provide copies of all the franchise contracts, agreements, etc.

- **Location documents:** If you are going to be leasing or buying a storefront, you will need to provide the proposed lease (for a rental) or purchase agreement (for a buy).

- **Résumés:** Most investors will want to know your past experience and abilities. Providing résumés for each business owner will help investors or bankers understand why you are qualified to own this business. Make sure to fine-tune your résumé to show how your past experience qualifies you for this business. For instance, if any of your past positions included managing technology equipment — even if it wasn't "officially" in your job description — make sure to include it on this version of your résumé!

- **Legal documents:** If you have mentioned any legal documents in the business plan (e.g., licenses, reseller certificates), you can include them in the supporting documents.

2. Choose Your Business Structure

Before you begin to practice as a computer repair and/or computer sales business, make sure you have your business details set up. You will need to complete all the different legal hurdles in your city, state or province, and country.

One of the biggest decisions that you will need to make is your business structure. Your choices include:

- **Sole proprietorship:** This is used to refer to a business with a single owner who does not set up a separate legal entity. The risk of this form is that if there is a lawsuit, *you*, not your company, can be held liable.

- **Partnership:** This includes two or more people as the owners of the business. It is similar to a sole proprietorship in that it is easy to set up and there are lower start-up costs. Also similar to the sole proprietorship is that you and your partner(s) can be held personally liable should there be a lawsuit. (See section **2.1** for important information about partnerships.)

- **Limited Liability Company (LLC) and Limited Liability Partnership (LLP):** These entities are often used by small-business owners. Unlike a sole proprietorship and partnership in which you are personally liable, an LLC or LLP has limited liability. This means that you are creating a new entity (the corporation) and if there is a lawsuit, it is the business, not you personally, that will be held liable. These entities have limited reporting, and taxes can be "passed through" to the owner instead of being taxed separately. One significant difference between LLCs and LLPs is that while an LLC can be formed by one owner, an LLP requires two or more owners.

- **S corporations and C corporations (in the US):** For a small-business owner, corporations can be a bit more complicated to manage and maintain. However, if you intend to grow using venture capital or eventually sell the business, this may be a better structure.

Incorporation is important for many reasons, but primarily it is a way to reduce your risk. You want to protect yourself from liability, especially when you're working in someone's office or home and run into a problem with the person's computer or data. However, it's not necessary to be officially incorporated to fix a person's computer. It is possible to start the business first, and incorporate later. Then, when things work well, and you decide this is the business you want to be in, you can incorporate. There are huge tax advantages and disadvantages for each so don't put this off too long. There are quite a few types of corporations and you want to choose the one that fits your business best.

There are many different resources available to help you choose your legal entity. If you aren't sure, you can always create an LLC and convert the business to an S corporation or a C corporation later (although you will need to pay legal and accounting fees). However, in the end, the best thing to do is to discuss your personal situation with your lawyer and accountant before you choose. Discussing it with both of them at the same time will help to reduce your risk, management overhead, and tax burden.

Depending on your state or province, the costs of incorporation can vary. The cost of creating an LLC on your own can be less than $200 but if you choose to get assistance from a lawyer, an accountant, or an on-site service the price can balloon to as much as $1,000.

Since the rules to create an entity will vary depending on your location it is generally worthwhile to do some research and get some professional advice before you file yourself. For instance, in Arizona, there is a two-page form that has to be filled out, notarized, and sent to the state. After that a notification needs to be published in an approved newspaper. However, in other states, such as Ohio, there is nothing more to do than fill out a short form.

> One of the most common structures used by small businesses in the US is a Limited Liability Company (LLC). They are easy to create, manage, operate, and taxes are relatively simple. If you are considering forming an LLC for your business, *How to Form and Operate a Limited Liability Company: A do-it-yourself guide*, by Gregory C. Damman will help you understand the ins and outs of forming and operating an LLC in your state and it will save you some money when you create your entity.

2.1 An important note about partnerships

Many people who consider creating a business often feel it would be easier to start a business with a partner than it would be to run the business alone. Having a partner can help the business grow for many reasons. A partner can provide a second perspective, more help running day-to-day operations, and invest financially, reducing the monetary burden of starting a new business. However, partnerships can be difficult because decision-making is not centralized, functions are distributed, and fights can ensue. Therefore, if you choose to run your business with another person, make sure to create a partnership agreement *before* you begin.

A partnership agreement is designed to include the expectations both partners have for each other. It should include details regarding:

- The term (duration) of the partnership

- Investment of capital (including whether interest will be paid on that capital)

- Profit and loss distribution

- Salaries

- Management duties and limitations

- Banking

- Termination clause — how the partnership will be dissolved and what happens to the business

- Death clause — information about what happens upon the death of a partner

- Arbitration — document fully how problems will be resolved

In some cases, you may want to include these items in the corporation documents instead of a separate partnership agreement, but your lawyer will be able to direct you to the correct format for your situation. Make sure you contact a lawyer to draw up a partnership agreement to protect all parties involved as well as the business. If the partnership goes sour, it can affect the business.

3. Apply for an Employee Identification Number or a Business Number

After your business is created, there is one more step that you should take — obtain an

Employee Identification Number (EIN) in the US, or a Business Number (BN) in Canada. This number will be used in the future for everything from tax filings to bank accounts.

In the US, the EIN is obtained directly from the Internal Revenue Service (IRS) and is free if you apply yourself online. The page is a little tricky to find since the URL is not simple: https://sa2.www4.irs.gov/modiein/individual/index.jsp.

Remember, creating an EIN is a legal obligation. Once you create your ID, the IRS will expect you to either file taxes or to at least cancel the EIN if you don't wind up using it.

In Canada, the BN can be applied for through the Canada Revenue Agency (CRA) at www.cra-arc.gc.ca/E/pbg/tf/rc1.

 Don't forget to look into business licenses and seller's permits for your area. Talk to your local city hall or business association in your area to find out more about the licenses and permits you may need as they vary from region to region.

4. Separate Your Business and Personal Assets

One thing many people don't realize is that creating a separate business entity isn't just about branding. The purpose of the entity is to protect you personally and provide you with limited liability in case of a lawsuit. However, creating a legal entity is not enough to protect you from legal consequences if your business runs into trouble. In order to keep your business a separate legal entity, you need to *always* treat it like a separate company. In short, this means you may not use the business as an extension of your personal finances. You can't just take $100 from the cash drawer and use it to buy yourself a new toy. You have to treat the corporation as if you do not own it. If that were the case, taking $100 would be stealing and you must know that the IRS takes this very seriously. If you don't keep the two separate, you can open yourself up to the consequences of a lawsuit.

Let's say you're working on someone's computer and his or her hard drive dies. The person tells you that all his or her information is on it and it's your fault the drive died. Even if it isn't your fault, the person can choose to sue you for loss of revenue, the cost of the drive, and anything his or her lawyer can think of. If you keep your personal finances separate from the business finances, the most the person can do is sue the business. If you haven't — if you've treated the business as your personal bank — the person's lawyer will argue that you didn't respect the legal corporate structure and this "pierces the corporate veil." If he or she is successful, you will be personally liable for everything the business is liable for and you can be personally sued for you assets, including your house, your car, any financial resources, and more.

In order to show that your business is separate from your personal life, you need to do the following:

- **Separate finances:** Once your business entity is created and you have an EIN or a BN, you should create an account at your local bank. All business expenses, payments, etc., should go through this account.

- **Separate taxes:** Make sure to tell your accountant that you have a new business and make sure that your taxes are filed.

- **Separate business space:** If you are going to work at your home, you should have a dedicated office space for your business. This space and the utilities to make it livable will then be tax deductible as a business expense.

- **Represent yourself as a business:** In general, you should represent yourself as a business, not as yourself. This means that all of your paperwork, business cards, emails, etc., should represent you as an employee of the business and not as Joe Smith.

If you always keep your company separate from your personal life, then you will be better prepared to defend your business as a separate entity. Once you start using your business to pay for personal expenses or mix your personal funds with your business funds, you will be proving that the business is not a separate entity and you will open yourself up for legal and personal consequences.

5. Insurance

Since you will be working on customer and business computers either at their locations or at your own, you will want to invest in insurance. Insurance will cover you in case there is a problem or you cause damage at a customer's site. The easiest way to get insurance is to contact a professional insurance broker who can find you insurance to meet your needs at a low cost.

Just because you have insurance doesn't mean you should use it frequently. We know one computer business that actually had to close its doors because of their insurance costs. They began with reasonable rates and a retail store.

Then there was a computer theft, which they reported to insurance and had insurance pay. A little while later, they lost a customer's data and instead of resolving it with the customer (which is possible) they simply handed the problem to their insurance company. Little by little, all of these claims caused their insurance rates to skyrocket. Soon, their insurance became unaffordable and since they had to pay it each month, it was dramatically reducing their profits. In the end, they closed their store. The moral of the story is that while insurance is important, it shouldn't be used too liberally if you want to keep low insurance rates.

Building Credibility

Before you start your advertising or even take on your first customer, you can begin to build your credibility. There are many things that you can do to create a business that customers will trust. Building your brand shows that you are a professional company that intends to be in business for the long haul.

1. Design a Logo

Do you need a logo? It certainly isn't critical but it can come in handy. Logos stick in people's minds and help identify your brand. Arizona Computer Outlets has a silly looking peach with its tongue sticking out (blame the old owners; we do). Do we like it? No. However, the customers remember it. People who haven't been to our store in years come back and look for that logo. A name can be forgotten, but a logo tends to stay with people.

Fortunately, in today's Internet world, you can get a professionally created logo that you provide feedback and guidance on for as little as $300. The website, LogoTournament.com, is a great place to get your design. All you do is put up your payment ($300) and describe what you are looking for (e.g., color scheme, style). Designers from around the world will help create an image that meets your expectations and will stick in customers' minds. Plus, during the "tournament" you can provide feedback to the designers. As each designer submits his or her entry, you can let them know how you feel about it. Soon, the logos start to get closer and closer to your ideal. By the time the tournament is over, you will have a logo that you love at a price you can afford.

2. Create a Professional Website

Another way to add credibility to your business is to develop a professional-looking web presence. A great website will bring in revenue and build your market reputation. You can direct your advertising traffic to the site by adding the URL to your business cards for those individuals who want additional information about you and your business. Also, when you are doing Internet advertising on sites such as Craigslist, you can use your website to store the images you will use in your ads.

Getting a website is relatively simple. It can be purchased through GoDaddy.com for less than $100 (including all the bells and whistles). In general, try to stay with a website that uses the .com extension and one that is easy to remember. While many companies use dashes and hyphens in their name, it is less confusing if you use an URL that is all one word. Our website address, www.ArizonaComputerOutlets.com may be long but since it matches our store name, it is easy to remember.

Get the Web Name Variations!

When you first purchase a website, you may be tempted to just buy the URL you need. When we bought the website for Arizona Computer Outlets, we made sure to get the full name of the business, www.ArizonaComputerOutlets.com and trademarked our name. However, it was still galling when another local computer store purchased the same domain name, only without the "s." So, plan ahead and get all the name variations that could steal your traffic.

2.1 Building your website

There are many ways to create a very professional looking website that is fast and easy to maintain. Even if you don't have a great deal of coding experience, it is now possible to build professional looking websites. If you choose to build the site yourself, there are many great options out there. The following are two tools which I have used before:

- **Go Daddy's Website Tonight:** If you want a supported website design, Go Daddy offers its "Website Tonight" product. This tool allows you to create a custom website based on hundreds of available templates with an infinite number of combinations. There is a monthly fee for this service, but it may be worthwhile if you want to have someone to call.

- **WordPress:** My current favorite is WordPress because it is easy to use, easy to manage, and continually updated with new plug-ins (i.e., pre-created tools that you can use on your website for free). In general, all the tools here are free and they can be downloaded to any hosting site (including GoDaddy). This is one of the least expensive options.

Of course, if you want your site to use flash intros or special shopping carts, it may be worthwhile to invest in a professionally built and managed site. Just be careful about investing too much money up front. While professional sites will look better, they may be harder to manage and update. So, if your business changes greatly in the first year or two, it may be expensive to keep your website up to date. In general, it's better to start cheaper (think free) and expand the site as your business grows. The temptation is to go with something fancy. After all, the business is a reflection of you, and the website is the customer's portal to your business. Remember our maxim: If it doesn't make you money and pay for itself, don't do it!

2.2 Critical information to include on your website

Once you have the basics of your website, you can begin to fill in the content. Some things that you may want to add to your website include:

- **Warranty information:** Include your service policy as well as the hardware policy. This lets people know that you stand behind your product and services.

- **Contact information:** Create a dedicated email address which matches your company website name (e.g., computertech@yourwebsite.com) not a generic Gmail or Yahoo! account. People tend to trust "real" email addresses more than the free ones. Whatever you do, don't use an AOL address. No one will take you seriously.

- **Product list:** If you sell used computers, make them available online. Although you may not get many sales like this you will get some. When we posted our products online we were surprised when we started to receive occasional orders in the first month with no advertising!

- **Feedback area:** Also known as a brag sheet, this is where you post all the great customer feedback that you receive. If you receive any supportive customer emails or thank-you notes, make a copy and post it! Just remember to respect your customers' privacy and don't use their full names without their written permission.

- **News and notices:** As a business owner, any coverage you receive from newspapers, websites, or magazines should always be posted directly on your website. You may not have any at first, but one public relations professional we met described this area as your pedigree to influence customer sales!

- **About you:** If you are running the business, include some information about yourself. You may want to mention your experience, training, certifications (if you have them), and other information that shows you are qualified to fix the customer's computer.

Brag! The more information you give about yourself, the more credibility you'll build and the less time you'll spend gaining the customer's trust.

- **Advice area:** Another way to show customers your professionalism is to include a few tips and tricks on your website. While you can create this yourself, you can also use tips from other sites (make sure to check the copyright information before you put anything on your site).

3. Vehicle Wrapping

If you plan to complete on-site jobs, you should have some way of distinguishing your vehicle as a company vehicle. This is not required, but it is a great way to increase your advertising (all the other cars on the road will see your signage). If you don't have a retail storefront, this makes you seem more professional when you arrive.

While a full wrap can set you back a few thousand dollars, doing the windows or doors professionally is usually much less. If you're spending an hour per day on the road, you're advertising your business at least one hour per day! Think about how much it would cost you to get an hour of radio or television advertising. Plus, you'll be shocked at how many calls you'll get. You need something catchy that people can remember and a simple phone number. You have about ten seconds to sell yourself and your business, so make it count!

The other option people often consider are two small magnets on either door. Let's face it, this rarely looks professional. If you choose to go this route, realize that little magnets on the door may get you some business, but only a little. Someone has to be parked next to you at a light to see them or has to stop and read it if you're parked. While this can be done professionally, most of the time, it looks temporary and people won't think your business is permanent. Also, it ruins the paint underneath the magnet, so think long and hard before you commit to doing this.

Whatever you choose, make sure that it is easy to read and easy to remember. Simple advertising will work best for your car since most of the people who see this advertising will be driving in their own cars and won't be able to take notes. Before you choose, look around at what other people are doing with their vehicles. You're not trying to blow their minds with your artistic ability, you're conveying information. Give them your name, your service, your competitive advantage, and a means of contact. They're not going to remember more than that anyway.

4. Professional Forms and Documents

This is another area some people try to skimp on. To save a few bucks, they often print forms directly from their computer instead of getting forms professionally created. This is a mistake. First, when you get forms professionally created, you have the option of getting carbonless forms. This means that you can have the customer write on the top copy (your copy) and then give them the bottom copy as their receipt. This ensures that you both have the same information of the work completed and appears more professional overall. Second, it ensures that you always have the forms that you need with you.

If you choose to order forms, keep your first set small. Inevitably, as you work with your customers, there are changes that you will wish you could make. Ordering a small

amount that you will go through quickly will let you get your second order right. Sure, a small order costs more, but using forms that are missing information or worse yet, throwing them out is significantly more expensive.

As always, you don't need to do this on Day 1. You can print out your own forms and documents until you get going, but you will spend the money in ink and paper plus you will lose the advantages a printed form provides.

5. Professional Business Cards

Even if you don't listen to me about the vehicle wraps and forms, please *don't* print your business cards on your printer. They look cheap and unprofessional. Worse yet, they look like you only thought of becoming a computer professional earlier that day and at the last minute decided to print off some cards. Especially if you are working out of your house, this could scare off customers. Spending a hundred dollars or so on business cards will be worthwhile advertising in the long run. There are plenty of online places that will print a few hundred cards for the cost of shipping, so take advantage of these services. Ink is expensive, so don't spend it on business cards.

One way to give out your business cards is to affix a small packet of cards to your vehicle's window. That way, when people are walking by your parked vehicle, they can grab a card for later. Make sure you have a giant arrow that points to it so people know it's there for them.

5.1 Critical information to include on a business card

Sometimes a business card is the only information a customer has about your business, so make sure the card is something of which you can be proud. The goal of your business card is to give your customers the information they need to contact you. Therefore, make sure your card is easy to read, clear, and concise. The following are some things you may want to include on your business card:

- **Certifications and specialized training:** While training isn't required to become a computer repair person, it is valuable to list any certifications that you have. As we've mentioned, the certifications won't really help you fix a computer, but customers love them and certifications build confidence.

- **Contact information:** Think about how you want to be found. In general, you should list any way a customer may want to contact you. This includes your business address, website, email address, phone number, fax number, emergency number, etc. Just remember, if you don't have a business address (or are working from your home) make sure that your phone number and email are prominently listed on your business card.

- **Logo:** It may seem silly, but people seem to think a company is more credible if it has its own logo, so add it to your business card.

At our store, we get a lot of people who have viruses. To remind them how to close windows without launching viruses, we created some business cards that have instructions for using Alt-F4 to close windows. This encourages customers to keep our business cards and hopefully the next time they have a more complex problem, they will still have our business card!

Once you figure out what to put on the card, make sure that the cards you pick have a decent paper weight. If the cards are too flimsy, they will seem cheap. If they are too "slick," it may make the customers wonder if your prices are too high. Finding a balance may take a while, but nice cards will be remembered by your customers.

 Make business cards people *want* to keep. As you work with more and more customers you will find that there are some questions people often ask. Create some specialized business cards that have answers to common questions on one side and your contact information on the other. This will make sure people keep your cards and have your information whenever they need it.

Free (or Almost Free) Advertising

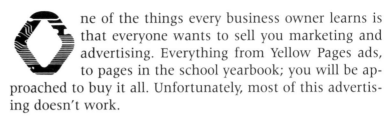ne of the things every business owner learns is that everyone wants to sell you marketing and advertising. Everything from Yellow Pages ads, to pages in the school yearbook; you will be approached to buy it all. Unfortunately, most of this advertising doesn't work.

At one time, we were paying more than $6,000 per month in advertising. We had multiple ads running in all the local papers, we had full-page ads in magazines, we were on the back of supermarket receipts, and even on bulletin boards at RV parks. We were skeptical that it was actually paying for itself so we took a month and asked every single person who walked in or called how they'd heard about us. We were astounded. The great majority had heard about us from friends or had just walked by. This ran counter to what we'd thought and when we ran the numbers we were just sick to our stomachs. The advertising generated many calls but it didn't translate into revenue. The issue we had was that people were calling from all over the valley and didn't want to drive 45 minutes to get their computers fixed when they could drive 3 minutes to a more local store. In addition, the calls chewed up most of the day so we found we were falling behind on actual work! Based on this, we dropped the advertising and, although our call volume declined, our profit remained about the same and we were able to get more work out the door.

As a new business owner, instead of spending thousands of dollars on advertising, take advantage of all the free advertising you can get. As soon as you launch, you will be deluged with people who want to sell you every kind of advertising under the sun. Don't be fooled. They will promise you the world and you'll rationalize and justify how spending a few hundred dollars will turn into many thousands of dollars in sales. It may, but it is not guaranteed. Once we sent out 280,000 flyers and got only *one* phone call.

Spend your time advertising for free. In the early stages of your business this is where you need to put your time, not in worrying that the thousand dollars you just spent was wasted. Free advertising includes, but isn't limited to, everything from websites to word of mouth. There are many resources you can use; this chapter includes the forms of advertising we like to use.

1. Creating Craigslist Ads

If you are looking for customers immediately, the fastest and least expensive place to advertise is Craigslist. This website allows you to post your ad for free; however, in most areas there is significant competition. In general, you should start these ads as soon as you launch your business. Some companies make a living from these ads alone. One computer store we know believes these ads are so valuable they have hired a part-time person who posts these ads for them every day.

Although Craigslist discourages you from putting up multiple ads, if you offer something different each day, you will be able to have your ads available regularly. Here are a few tips and tricks:

- Create multiple versions of the same ad. Craigslist will notice if you post the same ad over and over, but different ads with different wording will be accepted. Be careful, as competitors will flag your posts as unacceptable just to keep you from advertising services they provide.

- Reuse old ads. Craigslist lets you "renew" old ads, so you can just reuse postings again and again.

- Craigslist allows you to reference images on other sites. If you create a slick ad that is a .jpg, post it on your website and just reference it in the ad. The image will be displayed on Craigslist and Craigslist doesn't read it as a duplicate.

- Post at different times during the day. Craigslist can be cutthroat. Sometimes other companies will report your ads to discourage competition. Therefore, repost during various times of the day to ensure that you always have an ad available.

- There is software that your competition can purchase that will auto-flag posts with certain keywords. If you advertise "virus removal" and they are scanning for those keywords, your post will be auto-flagged and it will be removed minutes after you post. To avoid this, try to link images whenever possible.

- Don't get discouraged. Just because your first ad doesn't bring in any customers doesn't mean that you should stop. Sometimes it takes some ad "tuning" to find the right ad that will return results.

2. Investing in Happy Customers

Whatever your business sells, happy customers are always your best advertising. Typically they live in your area, they know other people who live near you, and often have friends and neighbors with similar problems. Happy customers like to recommend a new business because people feel good when they are able to talk about a great experience. Our business currently spends no money on monthly advertising and yet we get plenty of new customers. Almost all of them are recommendations from other people who had a great experience with us. This type of advertising is worth the time it takes to earn it.

There are plenty of ways to earn happy, excited customers. While it may take more time and effort, it is certainly worth the sales it generates. Some ways to get people excited about your business include:

- **Save your customers money.** Many businesses take advantage of ignorant customers to up sell unnecessary products and services. If your recommendations save your customers money, they will appreciate it and feel grateful. Letting them know you can fix their computer for $100 instead of selling them a new one for $400 may make you the same amount of money (typically new computers have low margins) but save the customers $300!

- **Be competitively priced and let your customers know it!** When you are saving them money, don't be afraid to let them know. Although you don't want to mention any company by name, you can mention the prices at the local big box store and let them know how much lower your prices are.

- **Thank your customers for their business.** Let them know how much you appreciate their patronage.

- **If your customers want to thank you, ask them to refer a friend.** We get customers that are so happy that we solved their problem that they want to do something nice for us or leave a tip. Instead of accepting a gift, we generally ask them to just refer a friend. Usually they will leave with a stack of cards in hand and a promise to give out the cards! You can't buy that type of advertising.

With that said, unhappy customers can sink your business. How often have you had a friend ask you about a local restaurant or store? You know that when you tell your friends about a terrible experience you had it stays with them. Unless it is unavoidable, always try to resolve problems with your customers to everyone's satisfaction. It used to be that 1 angry person would tell 10 to 20 people about his or her experience with a business. Now, that 1 person can spread negative comments much more. In a few seconds he or she can post to theripoffreport.com or yelp.com and when people search your name, the first thing they'll see is a bad report about you. Do everything you can to keep your customers happy.

3. Writing an Internet Blog

Posting new content on your website is a great way to get new hits — especially if you offer online sales. Even small articles on current events, new viruses, recently released computer games, or spotlights on new technology will help bring traffic to your site. This is an especially good thing to focus on when you are first building your business. Writing these articles will help you learn more about the industry and what customers are looking for. In general, try to update your blog daily. One way to do this is to read recent tech news and blog about it.

4. Social Media

Another way businesses generate traffic is through social media. This area has grown so large in recent years that you now have many different choices and methods of expanding your business with these free social sites. Some sites that you should consider include:

- **Facebook:** Create a page for your business. You can start managing updates that give your customers information about how your business is growing, any special deals or offers, or maybe just some tech tips.

- **Twitter:** These feeds allow you to send out updates to readers. As you are regularly working on repairs, you may find items of interest. Have you just found a new virus? Is there a new product release? Tweet about it!

- **Google:** Google often tracks business information and allows you to update your business information directly on its site. The more hits you get, the better. Recently, Google even sent a photographer to one of our stores to photograph it inside and out!

- **Merchant Circle, and other merchant groups:** Today, many merchant associations are forming. These websites usually allow you to create a page for your business for free and often let you link to other business in your area.

Take advantage of each of these sites to start creating buzz about your business or your services. When we started Computers for Soldiers, a charitable program that offers laptops and desktop computers at affordable prices for the military and their families, we started a Facebook page for the program. Since our program is about helping military families find affordable computers, we didn't sell the computers on our Facebook page. Most of our updates are about visiting military families, getting the word out on army bases, and getting feedback from our customers. What was amazing was how much excitement and traffic it generated.

Just remember to keep your web presence professional. Don't include cute stories about your pets or your kids and certainly don't get involved in "wars" with customers and competitors. Remember, the Internet is forever; once you hit submit, the comment you made will exist somewhere on the Internet.

Marketing in the New Media, by Holly Berkley: This book is a great start if you are looking for more information on how to market using the Internet and mobile media. It covers tips on using social marketing, boosting website traffic, and monitoring online customer behaviors.

5. Networking with Complementary Businesses

If you choose to open a retail location, you can network with other business owners in your area. If you are working from home, why not try to do the same thing? Get to know your neighbors and the businesses in your immediate area. Walk around, talk to people, ask them how their systems are running, and just be friendly and approachable.

Take every chance to tell people about your business. For instance, the other day I was in a small coffee shop doing some writing. I asked the owner if she had wireless access for customers and couldn't believe how convoluted it was to connect. She started telling me about all the problems they had been having, how they couldn't even change the access credentials to something simple, and people had to input a long alphanumeric string to connect. Of course, I offered to help. A few minutes later, I had her network back together and she was thrilled. Now, was it profitable? A little bit; she gave me a free coffee and soup, but most importantly, she now knows that I am a technician who can solve problems quickly and easily. Taking advantage of opportunities like this builds your reputation in the business community quickly.

Another way to grow in your community is to get involved with a local charity. Donating your time is a free way to get some publicity for your business. Even if it doesn't result in any sales, you can use these experiences to build your online and in-store reputation. If you are at a charity event or donate an item, add that to your website. If charity organizers thank you with a plaque or certificate, hang it in your business and make a copy available on your website. While these activities may not result in immediate direct sales, it will build your reputation and show your customers that you are reliable and caring.

6. Paid Advertising

There are many business owners who swear that their advertising keeps them in business. The key is to know what advertising costs and what it brings in. Before you buy any advertising, you need to make sure the vendor can show you how many people actually read its advertising (versus how many people "could" read it) and what the results are like for businesses like yours.

Keep in mind, vendors will exaggerate. If the advertising salesperson tells you the vendor has a circulation of 50,000, ask him or her what that means. Is the circulation in your immediate area? If your business targets families, does the advertising go to neighborhood homes or is it distributed at college campuses? Make sure that the advertising is actually going to be distributed to your customer base. Many times, we've seen stacks of magazines in a garbage and wondered how much people paid to advertise with them. Be very careful. Ask to speak to other people who advertise with them. Make sure you aren't competing against multiple businesses like yours.

If, after all your research, you think that a particular type of advertising is for you, begin

working on the right ad. The content of the ad often makes a big difference in the results. For instance, if an ad is too wordy, some people don't even bother to read it. If an ad looks too unprofessional, people may doubt the quality of your computers and your service. Therefore, spend the time to make your ad look professional. Get as much feedback as you can before you ever run the ad. Ask your friends, family, and customers and listen to their feedback. Ask them for candid feedback and never be insulted by their responses. After all, you want an ad that sells.

Another thing to consider is tracking. Once the ad is running you will need a way to measure the results; therefore, include a "call to action" in the advertisement. For instance, asking the customer to "bring in this coupon" is an easy way to know that your advertising worked. If you are doing Internet advertising, provide a link to a custom-made page or create a custom email address so that you can track every single response or hit.

Once you have an ad that appears to work, continue to fine tune it and track results. Change small elements and try to improve your sales. If most of your customers are calling about your laptops, see what happens when your ad dedicates more space to selling your laptops. Whatever you do, continue to measure not just hits (e.g., calls) but also sales. We had one ad, a newspaper classified, that resulted in many phone calls, but little to no sales. As a result, we not only spent money on the ad, but we spent our time fielding calls from people that lived too far away to become customers.

Do *not* sign a long-term contract. Salespeople will suggest you advertise with their vendor for six months as if that were a short period of time. It isn't. Try for a month and track the results. If the salesperson won't let you test the results, he or she doesn't have confidence in his or her product. If the salesperson truly believes you'll be successful through his or her vendor, the person will have no objection to you trying it. If it brings in customers, keep going! If not, drop it and try something else.

5

Tools of
the Trade

unning a computer repair business should be a very low-cost endeavor. Unfortunately, we have seen many people who spent so much money starting a business that it was nearly impossible to sustain the company. One example is a new computer store that took more than six months to build the interior of their building. This means that the owners had the business (e.g., paying rent, utilities) for six months before they ever opened the store for customers! When they finally opened their doors, it was a disaster.

The owners spent a fortune on the design and layout of the interior. It had gorgeous wooden floors, which looked very nice, but hard floors will break any parts that may happen to fall on them. The store had a beautiful desk for computer repair but the back was closed off. The techs only had access to one side of the systems and the computers were in the enclosed space, which meant the computers would overheat.

Another problem the store had was that customers couldn't see the store from the road and there wasn't any parking. It was as if whoever built the store bought a manual on how to do everything wrong and followed it to the letter.

We felt really badly for them but the worst part was that they had spent so much on remodeling and carrying costs that they had no money to survive until they could become profitable. We found out about them because less than three months after they opened, the business was for sale.

When you decide to start your business, all your decisions should be made to obtain the highest possible value for the lowest possible cost. You can always invest in different technologies and equipment as the business grows, but before that, the lower the costs, the better.

1. Software You Should Own

In general, you want to own any software you use. What I mean by this is that you should not be using pirated versions of any software even if it is a widely accepted practice. While it may cost more up front, the security it provides your business is worthwhile.

1.1 Microsoft TechNet and Microsoft Action Pack

The Microsoft TechNet and Microsoft Action Pack are definitely worthwhile products. The Microsoft Action Pack will give you dozens of licenses to set up your business, from Windows to Server 2008. Get it. You will not regret it.

TechNet will give you the rest of what you will need such as downloadable copies of every OS ever sold, including DOS 6.22 and early versions of Windows. It is absolutely imperative that you have access to this. If you don't, you'll end up trying to torrent one online and hoping it isn't riddled with viruses. When someone brings you an odd tablet computer with a strange OS, you can just download it, burn a disk, and reload his or her OS with no trouble.

1.2 LogMeIn Rescue

If you plan to do any type of computer repairs, LogMeIn Rescue is a must-have. This product allows you to log into another individual's computer and take control. Take a look at the following two examples:

- A customer calls you complaining about a recent repair. If he or she can connect to the Internet, you can look at the computer together. We have had many situations when the problem the customer is concerned about either doesn't exist or is easy to fix. Either way, LogMeIn Rescue saves you or your customer a trip. The way it works is you tell your customer to go to www.logmein123.com. When he or she does, you'll log into your console, and generate a six-digit PIN which is used to allow you access. The PIN is only good for 20 minutes but if you log into the customer's computer during that time, you will be working on it as if you

were sitting in front of it. This tool is amazing and we use it daily.

- A customer asks for a new service call. Instead of traveling immediately to the site, you can ask if she wants the service call completed over the phone. Without leaving your home or business, you can complete many types of repairs. If you offer a lower rate (e.g., $20 or even $30 off per hour), your customer will probably go for it and you will be able to multitask while you complete repairs.

Although the software costs about $100 per month, the cost is offset by the work you will be able to complete by using it and the customer complaints you can resolve. Even if you only use the software to deal with customer complaints, it is a worthwhile tool to have because it will increase customer satisfaction and happy customers build business!

1.3 Accounting software

Before you get too far in your business, you need to obtain accounting software. While there are many expensive products (e.g., QuickBooks) on the market, you can also find less expensive and sometimes even shareware solutions. Finding software that you can use to track all your expenses, send out invoices, and track inventory will be beneficial in the long run.

Bookkeepers' Boot Camp: Get a grip on accounting basics, by Angie Mohr: If you choose to do your books yourself (and it may be worthwhile in the beginning) this book will help you learn what to track, how to track it, and how to understand it. With detailed instructions on all the financial statements and tracking your business needs, this book is a good way to get started being your own bookkeeper.

1.4 OpenOffice

Considering the cost of Microsoft Office (one license can be more than $100) there may be times that you want to open files and don't necessarily want a full license of Microsoft Office on your machine. A great free alternative is OpenOffice. This product will allow you to open most files created in the Microsoft suite without paying for a full Microsoft installation. Of course, if you purchase the Microsoft Action Pack, you won't need to buy this because it provides you with ten licenses.

1.5 Norton Ghost

Keep images of your computers. You know this already, but it can't be stressed enough. Computers regularly have hard drive failures, blown power supplies, and viruses, so make sure to keep an image of all your work computers. Since your machines are going to be used regularly and connected with customer systems, you will probably find yourself wiping and reloading them more often than before. Keeping an image on hand will make this job easier. Once your workstation is configured the way you like, use Norton Ghost and create a full clone of the disk. Store it safely and when you need it, you won't have to waste hours getting your system back to where it was.

2. Necessary Websites

Have you ever installed a product onto your computer and gotten frustrated at all the extra software you still need? Most systems don't come pre-installed with Flash, Java, and a host of other useful tools. One company has built the solution. Ninite (www.Ninite.com) is a great way to complete installations of groups of products all at once. Just click on the software you want to install and select "install" at the bottom of the page. After that, the installations

are automatic. This is a great site to use to help you set up your work machines — especially after a wipe and reload. Keep in mind that they do have licensing requirements that you may need to look into if you are charging for the installation of any of these products.

If you have ever purchased a new computer from a big-box store, you know that they put every piece of software under the sun on that computer. The downside is that it is all trial software. This means that although they will not function after 30, 60, or 90 days, they continue to be loaded every time the computer is turned on, consuming memory and slowing down the computer. One way to fix this problem fast is the tool called the PC Decrapifier (www.pcdecrapifier.com). This great site lets you remove all the junk on the computer without much fuss and trouble.

Looking for a program or application? CNET (www.cnet.com) is the place to go. With the latest downloads for all major programs, this site is a great place to find the applications you need when you need them.

3. Your Work Area

Not everyone who chooses to run a computer repair business will need a retail location or commercial office space, but everyone should have at least one space that can be used exclusively for computer repairs. This area should contain everything you need to repair computers. However, don't get carried away. The less you spend on your setup the better. Remember, you are in this business to make money!

3.1 Inexpensive tech benches

There are many types of benches available, but the least expensive and simplest solution is what our stores use. Rather than spending money on high-end benches that can cost several hundred dollars, we buy inexpensive "gorilla" racks from hardware or office super stores. These benches are sturdy and give you access to the back and front of the computer. If you are going to complete repairs on multiple computers at once, these racks are a must have!

Eventually you may want enough space for 16 computers (this is usually about three, four-foot long shelves); at first, you should be able to get away with just one or two shelves.

3.2 The necessities

Once you have the benches, the next thing to set up is your workstation. You want your station to be easy for you to use, comfortable and convenient. To do this right, you will need the following:

- **One large monitor:** Make sure the screen is easy to read and not too small. Remember, you will be using it all day long.

- **Research computer:** In general, you need a computer that you can use to research problems, write customer estimates, etc. This computer should *never* be connected to any other customer computer to prevent it from getting infected with viruses.

- **Keyboard and mouse:** Make sure these are comfortable for you.

- **Uninterruptable power supply with automatic voltage regulation:** A UPS is even better than a surge protector. You should be using a voltage regulator to protect your customers' machines.

- **Printer**

- **Data transfer server:** This isn't strictly necessary, but it's extremely useful when you're working on transferring multiple customers' data at once. Our store can handle seven concurrent data transfers to one computer.

- **1- to 16-port switch box:** In general, one tech can handle about eight computers for repair and another five to six if they are used computers that are being wiped and reloaded. The workstation should have enough space for at least this many computers. I buy port switch boxes on Craigslist for less than a hundred dollars. There are some very sophisticated ones out there and eventually you may want to upgrade, but save yourself some money and start out with the less expensive ones.

  The great thing about switch boxes is that they allow you to multitask easily. With just one switch box, you can work on eight different computers at the same time. As your business grows, this will be required. For instance, repairs such as virus removals and OS installations can take hours to complete. During a great deal of this time, the computer is simply running with no input from the technician. Using a switch box allows the technician to sit in one place and move all the computers along.

As a computer repair business, you are going to need many types of screwdrivers including:

- **Power screwdrivers:** While you don't want to use power screwdrivers for laptop repair, having one handy is a lifesaver when you are building or repairing desktop computers.

- **Fine screwdriver set:** Even if you don't intend to complete laptop hardware repair, you will need a set of small screwdrivers to open and close laptops (e.g., RAM and hard drive upgrades).

- **Manual screwdriver set:** For when you don't want to use the power screwdriver.

- **A power supply tester:** The tester makes it easy to find one of the most common reasons why a computer simply won't turn on. All you do is unplug the big flat cable from the motherboard and plug it into this device. Green is good, red is bad, and yellow is bad. It's so simple and you've just figured out your problem. They're inexpensive to buy — about ten dollars — so it's worth having one in your office and one in your on-site equipment bag.

It is also important to have the technician tools you will use every day:

- **Large flash drive:** One of the easiest ways to transfer files is to use a flash drive. Investing in a large flash drive will give you enough room for all your common files and a few specialized applications as well. Note that they can get corrupted, so always back them up.

- **Blank CDs and DVDs:** As you troubleshoot, there will be times you want to transfer files from one computer to another. Keeping these disks handy will make life easier (look for sales at large office superstores to save a bundle).

- **External CD/DVD drive:** Occasionally you will find computers that have failing CD/DVD drives or possibly no drive at all. Having an external CD/DVD drive will let

you test these computers without much hassle. You are going to have to boot off of a CD in many cases and if the drive is broken, you'll be out of luck.

While you may not need these parts immediately, you may find times when you wish you had them to work on a customer's system:

- USB/PS2 converters for keyboards and mice

- VGA to DVI converters

- Universal laptop power adapter

- Thermal compound (Arctic Silver works well)

4. Payment Options

Once you start your business, you will have to choose what methods of payment you'll accept. If you require "cash only," you are guaranteed your money, but you are providing less flexibility; for example, some small businesses will not be comfortable paying in cash only. However, if you accept other types of payments you will either incur fees, take a risk on not getting your money, or both.

4.1 Checks

The general rule of thumb is that most businesses now don't accept checks. There is simply too much fraud with bounced checks. Even companies that have been in business for years will sometimes bounce a check and the cost to your company can be significant. Many times your bank will charge you a bounced check fee and then you must try to get the funds plus the fees. As a result, you can be working hard to get a check to cash properly.

4.2 Money orders and cashier's checks

While money orders and cashier's checks used to be trusted payment methods, today, they have become synonymous with Internet scams. People who pay with these items sometimes request "cash back" and then the payment bounces as well. Do not consider the bill paid until the money order or cashier's check has had time to clear.

4.3 Credit card machines

The standard credit card machines that we have seen all over are relatively simple to use and operate. The easiest way to get one of these is to call your bank and find out if there are any vendors that it recommends. Compare all the rates, pricing, and obligations. Depending on which company you go with your rates can change dramatically.

Also, read the fine print in your agreement! A low rate doesn't mean you'll necessarily save money. If you do many small transactions, you'll get hammered by the per-transaction fees.

4.4 PayPal

If you don't feel like investing in a credit card machine, you can always use PayPal as a simple substitute. With PayPal, you can charge your customers for work and even email them a receipt. The easiest way to set this up is with a simple website form that you can use yourself.

There are more downsides than we have time to go through, but there are three major reasons *not* to use PayPal so be very careful if you choose to use it:

- PayPal can hold your money whenever it wants.

- PayPal favors the customer and will simply refund the customer's payment no matter what you say.

- PayPal can cancel your account with no warning.

4.5 Barter

One of the most fun ways to do business is through barter. Today there are many different barter agencies around the country that help you find other companies who are interested in bartering. What's amazing about barter is that even when people are reluctant to spend actual dollars, they are ready to trade goods and services on barter.

Here's how bartering works: I sign up with a barter agency in my area (we use Value Card Alliance). We advertise our services. People who have also signed up (all types of businesses) contact me to purchase services. They pay me in "barter dollars" and those are applied to my account with a Value Card. The more work I do through this agency, the more barter dollars I accrue. I can use those on any of the goods and services offered by members of the agency.

When you're starting a business, this service can be particularly valuable. Let's say you're going to start a mobile computer repair service. You join the barter agency and put out a free ad on its site that you'd be thrilled to come and work on someone's system. You get a few calls, make a few barter bucks, then you trade the barter bucks in for one of the lawyers to create your company, one of the many printing companies to make your business cards, one of the sign-makers to create your signs, one of the graphic artists to create a logo for you, or one of the web designers to make your website. It's amazing how many different ways you can spend barter dollars.

Services

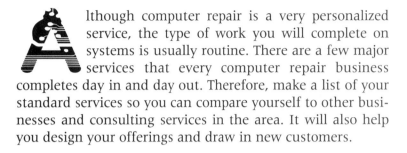lthough computer repair is a very personalized service, the type of work you will complete on systems is usually routine. There are a few major services that every computer repair business completes day in and day out. Therefore, make a list of your standard services so you can compare yourself to other businesses and consulting services in the area. It will also help you design your offerings and draw in new customers.

1. The Diagnostic

The first service any computer repair business has to think about is its diagnostic service. For many businesses, this is the service that brings customers to your company. At our retail locations, we offer a *"Free* in-store 15-minute diagnostic." This means that any customer who walks in can bring in his or her computer and find out what's wrong with it for free! As a result, we get many customers coming to us instead of going to another business.

In order to be able to offer this service for free, we generally restrict the tests to those a technician can run in about 15 minutes. Now, that doesn't mean that the customer will have the diagnosis 15 minutes after he or she enters the store, although we've had a customer or two over the years who tried to hold us to that interpretation. In some cases, the tests we run on a computer can take hours, but because we aren't working with the machine during that time (we just set it up and kick off the test) it is still included in the free diagnostic.

Other companies feel that giving away this service is not cost effective. Instead, they offer a *free* diagnostic on the condition that work is performed. For example, if they diagnose a bad hard drive and you agree to have them replace the drive, then the diagnostic was free. If you choose to have no work done, then you owe them $40. While this is a great way to advertise and get customers in the door you have to be up front about the charge. We have had some customers complain about businesses like these because they felt they were tricked into paying for a service they thought was free.

Some companies offer the diagnostic as just another service. Big-box stores have been known to charge as much as $80 to tell a customer that his or her computer was just not worth fixing. If you choose to go this route make sure you are up front with the customer before the diagnostic is performed.

In general, about 99 percent of our customers get a full diagnosis for *free*. However, there are three types of diagnostic requests (discussed in sections **1.1**, **1.2**, and **1.3**) that will cause us to request an extended diagnostic fee if the customer is interested in getting this type of customized information.

1.1 Custom estimate for laptop hardware repair

In general, we can usually provide a repair estimate on a broken laptop without taking apart the computer. However, if the customer wants us to take it apart and provide an exact estimate, we charge an extended diagnostic fee that can be applied to the service if he or she chooses to have the laptop repaired. The reason we charge for this service is that any technician needs dedicated time to take a laptop apart, find the part numbers, look them up online, and then put the entire system back together again. Because this is so time-consuming, we need to be paid for this effort.

1.2 Full diagnostic after multiple problems have been identified

In general, once we know a computer isn't worth repairing, we consider the free diagnostic done. Otherwise, since it is free, customers will want us to spend hours of our time to test every single part. For instance, one customer brought in an old computer with a bad power supply, a motherboard with bulging capacitors, and just 256K of RAM. We recommended that it wasn't worth fixing because a better, refurbished system would cost less than fixing the old computer. However, he still wanted to have

us run tests on all the parts of the computer just to find out if anything could be salvaged. We agreed we could test the system, but it would cost an extended diagnostic fee. He changed his mind and said, "Well, the parts are probably all bad because it has been in my garage for the last few years and I think my neighbor dropped a can of soda into it!"

1.3 Reproduction of intermittent errors

Occasionally, we get computers that have no signs of a problem. The customer may occasionally get an error but there is no way to reproduce it. In this case, if the computer tests out as working and the customer wants us to explore the problem in more detail, we will charge an extended diagnostic fee. However, we usually recommend that the customer use the computer a while longer and take notes every time the error is found. After a week or so of keeping this log, if he or she brings it back, it is much more likely that we can reproduce the issues without having to charge the fee.

2. Other Common Services

Choosing the services your business will offer is the foundation of your service price list (see Chapter 7 for more information about pricing). The most common services that your customers request should form the basis of this list and having this list will make it easier for you to make customer recommendations, quote prices, and even provide estimates.

Most computer repair businesses have services in common. The following sections look at the most common types of repairs as well as the tips, tricks, and pitfalls associated with each.

2.1 Tune-up

A tune-up is one of the simplest services you can offer. Typically customers need a few simple things done to their computer that will speed it up and get it running right. The following are some of the services that we include in a tune-up:

- Defragging the hard drive

- Getting and installing all Windows updates

- Validating that antivirus is correctly installed and working

- Shutting off unnecessary services and applications that are running in the background every time the computer starts up

- Checking virtual memory settings

At our store, we don't require any special paperwork to complete a tune-up because there should not be any special modifications made to the customer's computer that he or she needs to be aware of. Instead, our normal policy covers most of the risks and functions associated with this type of work.

To make sure that you complete the right tasks for a tune-up every single time, it helps to keep a checklist that you can use on each computer. Since technology changes quickly, you may want to use our tune-up checklist (see Checklist 1). However, you will need to update this regularly as new technology becomes available or as you find better, faster methods of completing repairs.

Checklist 1 is also included on the CD for you to modify and use in your business.

2.2 Virus removal

Unfortunately viruses are one of the most common problems facing computer systems today. The problems viruses can create range from slowing down the system (for the more innocuous bugs) to stealing all the banking information (for the more extreme items).

In general, virus removals are too time-consuming to complete on-site. A thorough virus removal will require you to scan the computer multiple times using many different tools before the viruses are truly gone. Therefore, to do this on-site is often too costly to be affordable (imagine paying for 15 hours of on-site labor to remove a virus). For both our business and private customers we recommend allowing us to do a virus removal at our location. This lets us work on multiple computers at once and gives us the time to remove the virus as thoroughly as possible. We charge a simple flat rate for the service.

2.2a Antivirus programs

There are many antivirus programs and they each change month-to-month and year-to-year. Most customers want to know the best product on the market, and although many are very good, no antivirus can stop every virus out there. Therefore, we tell our customers that the best way to prevent viruses is to learn good surfing habits which include:

- In Google searches, stay away from sites that you don't recognize. Obtaining information directly from the vendor is preferable to another third-party site.

- Don't click anywhere on a pop-up. Use Alt-F4 to close the pop-up without launching any code in the window.

CHECKLIST 1
TUNE-UP

Steps for a Tune-up	Completed
Clean out temporary files	
Shut off unnecessary services and remove old items from start-up (make sure to leave printer services active)	
Perform system defrag	
Check for operating system updates	
Check for active antivirus	
Blow out dust inside computer	

• Don't download software based on a pop-up or (in general) any software that you don't know.

There are always free and paid antivirus programs. While some are good and some are bad, there is no way to universally recommend one or the other forever. In our company, we changed our recommendation over the years to match the latest industry information. Depending on the year, we have recommended and sold about five different products. In general, this is an issue you will have to keep up on regularly, and update your customers on as well.

However, when your customer asks you to recommend an antivirus program, always go with a supported, paid product. The reason is the customer has someone to go to for help, questions, and complaints — and that person isn't you! When you recommend a large company such as Kaspersky Lab, McAfee, or Norton, the customer is buying a product from another vendor. When something goes wrong, and his or her computer gets a virus, or he or she has a problem with the installation, there is someone to call.

When you recommend a free product, odds are there is no formal support. As a result,

guess who gets the calls? You do. Why? Because you tried to save the customer a few bucks. If it goes wrong, guess who gets the blame? You do, again. When it works, guess what? No one cares. Another benefit of finding a paid product that you like is that you can usually sell this product to your customers and even add a service fee for the installation!

One thing we have learned through trial and error is to *never* install or recommend a free software package even if the customer asks for it and is willing to pay for the install. For some reason, once you do the installation — especially if you charge for the install — the customer will believe that you are supporting the product.

2.2b Virus removals are *not* included in the regular service warranty

You cannot warranty virus work. Because customers can get viruses at any time there is no way to ever guarantee that a virus removal will remain "clean." Don't even try. A company that guarantees this work could find itself fixing the same computer week after week for free. As a matter of fact, the few times we have helped a customer by "re-removing" viruses, it has caused more problems than it cured. One customer had a virus removal and came back a few days later saying the virus wasn't properly removed. Although we knew it was a recurrence, we removed it because it was so close together. A couple weeks later, she was back again with the same problem. When we wouldn't complete another free virus removal she was upset and started causing a scene. Explaining up front that virus removals can never be guaranteed is always easier than dealing with a hostile customer.

To prevent this problem, you need to follow these steps when you complete a virus removal check:

1. Check that the customers have antivirus. In general, all customers should be running some sort of antivirus program. If they don't have antivirus (or if it was corrupted by the virus or virus removal) —

   • let them know they don't have any active antivirus on their computer,

   • make it clear that a lack of antivirus opens up the computer to all sorts of problems and they will most likely get viruses again, and

   • offer to sell them an antivirus program.

2. Educate the customers about viruses — how a computer gets infected and how to prevent them. Remind them that sites which support music and movie pirating are also notorious for promoting viruses.

3. Have the customers try the machine in your shop as part of the check-out procedure. Then you both will know that the computer was working when he or she left.

4. If the customers have any problems, tell them to call immediately (i.e., within the first 24 hours) and explain that any problem found beyond that time could be the result of them getting another, new virus, so there will be no guarantee on the removal beyond that point.

In general, we have found that customers are very accepting about this. Because these rules have been explained up front, there is no confusion later on. Occasionally a customer will indicate that he or she doesn't have time to check the computer for a few days — at that point, you can decide if you want to extend the warranty (we usually do).

Sample 1 is an example of a virus removal agreement that we use with our customers. A version of this form is included on the CD to help you create your own agreement.

After printing the Virus Removal Agreement from the CD, you may want to print the Virus Removal Checklist (see Checklist 2) which you can then use to walk through the virus removals.

Since virus removals typically take a few days to complete it is important to track every task you do as you do it so that you don't lose track of where you are. Since these tasks may be different depending on what tools you use or how you like to do your virus removals, make sure to customize Checklist 2 before you use it. The checklist assumes that you do not have a separate virus removal server and are completing virus removals on the customer's computer.

Check-in Date [   ]

Virus Removal Agreement

Please fill out the information below. You must read and sign this work order before any work can begin.

PLEASE READ AND SIGN

If you choose to have us attempt to save all your files, YCOS will go through the following process:

- Remove hard drive from your machine and put into our machine dedicated to virus removal.
- Clean and/or delete any infected files.
- Purge operating system restore directories (roll back) and any identifiable third-party software restore. Restore files are often the first attacked and corrupted by today's viruses, and if left in system, any subsequent restores done accessing these files could cause the machine to be re-infected.
- Reassemble your system and check for functionality.
- Perform overlay and Winsock Repair, if applicable (this would incur an extra $49.00 fee. Virus may have affected operating system files and general functioning of the computer).

Understand that if key system files, such as registry files, have been corrupted by the virus, your system may still, ultimately, require a wipe and reload to restore it to full operating system integrity. (We would do this service at no additional charge.)

Some viruses can damage your system's hardware; even full removal of a virus cannot guarantee that your hardware will function as well as it did before virus infection.

Your Computer Outlet Stores (YCOS) is not liable for any data lost in the attempts to remove your virus.

I have read and understand the Virus Removal Agreement provided to me by YCOS. I give permission to YCOS to proceed with the following work action. I understand that I am responsible for associated charges and labor even if, for reasons outside of YCOS's direct control, virus removal is not entirely successful.

I understand that the virus removal process will stress the hard drive considerably beyond standard daily use. It will be running at 100% utilization while multiple programs scan and remove viruses, therefore any weaknesses in the drive may be exposed through the heavy load. Although rare, it is possible for a drive to fail mechanically during this process. If this happens, ALL DATA WILL BE LOST and the drive will be rendered inoperable.

Remove virus while attempting to save all files: $149.00 Charge

Possible additional $49.00 charge if, after removing the virus, Windows Operating System has been so corrupted by the virus that OS needs repair.

Customer Name (Printed): _____
Customer Signature: _____
YCOS Rep. Printed: _____
YCOS Signature: _____
Date: _____

CHECKLIST 2
VIRUS REMOVAL

Steps for a Virus Removal	Completed
1. Boot into safe mode	
2. Delete temporary files	
3. Disable system restore	
4. Install virus scanner 1 (choose your tool)	
5. Install virus scanner 2 (choose your tool)	
6. Run virus scanner 1 (record number of viruses)	
7. Run virus scanner 2 (record number of viruses)	
Note: At this point, repeat steps 6 and 7 until no new viruses are found. Both tools need to return zero viruses before you should move on.	

2.2c Answering the "porn" question

At some point you will receive the age-old question: "Why is there porn on my computer?" We all know that people watch porn. Some of our customers are really open about it. One actually asked us to make sure to back up his entire collection before we did any work. However, this is not the norm. Most people are very embarrassed about you finding any porn on their computer and are even more upset when they find it on someone else's computer (e.g., spouse, boyfriend, child). In some cases, the files have been added by viruses; however, if we are being candid, in most cases it has been downloaded by the user. The thing is, it is nearly impossible to tell which is which and as a computer business owner, it is not your job to speculate.

Occasionally, we get a mad spouse in the store who wants to know if the virus is from "watching porn" or some other such question. Each time we answer honestly; there is no way to know for certain how a virus/porn was obtained, but you can get them from anything and any site. Even if the question seems innocent, we still don't make any generalizations. After all, computer repair stores exist to fix broken computers, not to begin or end marriages!

2.3 Wipe and reload

One of the easiest functions to complete is a wipe and reload. Usually this is done when a computer's operating system is corrupted, or when a virus is so bad that it can't be removed.

2.3a Find the operating system key

Before you offer this service to a customer, make sure the customer has a legal operating system (OS) key. The only way you know an OS is legal is to find the certificate of authenticity (COA) either on the machine or to have a customer bring in the key. It has always amazed me how many people use pirated versions of their OS. If you start the installation and then realize the key is missing, the customer may become frustrated to discover he or she needs to spend more money on a new OS. Or, the customer may try to convince you to reinstall the illegal version he or she used to have (which you should never do).

> We all know how to grab the OS key out of the registry, but chances are if you have to get the key this way, it is not a legal operating system. The only way to be sure that your customer has a real, legitimate operating system is to see the key yourself. If you can't see it, don't install it.

2.3b Be clear

Make sure the customer understands what is going to happen. The problem with the wipe and reload is that the customer loses everything (e.g., photos, applications, data) and often doesn't understand what that means. Whenever you are reinstalling the OS, make sure to be *very* clear with the customer what will be lost and why the work is being completed. Go overboard on this explanation and make sure that the *customer* can clearly explain to *you* that he or she understands all of his or her data is being lost. If he or she can clearly say what is he or she is losing and is okay with that, you know the person understands what is happening.

One of the easiest ways to do this is to read them your wipe and reload agreement *before* they sign it. (See Sample 2.)

Some customers are okay with losing their data but would prefer to keep a copy. Make sure that your customers know that this is an option. Not only will they be happy to have the choice, but you can make another service sale: a data transfer!

2.3c Up sell a better OS

Another option that you can offer during a wipe and reload is to upgrade the customer's operating system. With Microsoft releasing new operating systems every few years, you may find that some customers are still on older operating systems, even if there is a better one on the market. Offering this type of upgrade will help both the customer and you.

For instance, in 2011, there are still customers that have XP or Vista instead of Windows 7. While both operating systems are fine, Windows 7 does have some benefits that make customers with newer computers interested in upgrading. From a customer perspective, a wipe and reload may be a perfect time to get the newest operating system. From a tech perspective, offering an upgrade to Windows 7 is another way to save you time and problems. Even if you offer the Windows 7 OS at your cost, the installation will be much faster than if you were installing and finding drivers for Vista or even XP. Therefore you can save time and make the same amount of money — a win-win situation for you and your customers.

Although wipes and reloads are one of the most fundamental functions, it is still important to follow a checklist to ensure all steps are complete (see Checklist 3). At our store, a technician may handle as many as 20 different systems in a given day; therefore, even simple tasks could be overlooked if they weren't properly tracked.

2.4 Data transfers versus data recoveries

Most people don't come in for data transfers just to move information from one machine to another. With the advent of large flash drives, DVDs, and off-site backups, more and more people complete their own data transfers and data backups. Therefore, the usual time that people want a data transfer is when their hard drive is failing. This means that they are already having problems with the computer, files aren't being read, the computer has blue-screened a

SAMPLE 2
WIPE AND RELOAD AGREEMENT

Check-in Date [   ]

Wipe and Reload Agreement

Please fill out the information below. You must read and sign this work order before any work can begin.

During a Wipe and Reload: **NO DATA AND NO PROGRAMS WILL BE SAVED.** All files will be deleted. All programs will be deleted.

- **All data will be deleted:** This includes all photographs, documents, files, browser bookmarks, Outlook emails, etc. No data that was stored on the computer will be saved during a wipe and reload.

- **All programs will be deleted:** This includes any games, financial software, downloaded applications, antivirus, etc. All "programs" located under the start menu will be removed. Programs must be reinstalled from the original installation CDs.

- **Microsoft Operating System will be reinstalled:** Microsoft operating system will not be "copied." During a wipe and reload, we will reload your operating system. You will probably not need the original disks; however, you will need your legitimate MS operating system (OS) key, also known as Certificate of Authenticity (COA), which will typically be taped to your computer. If you do not have this key, you will need to purchase a new copy of your operating system in order to reinstall this application.

Customer Name (Printed): _____

Customer Signature: _____

YCOS Rep. Printed: _____

YCOS Signature: _____

Date: _____

PLEASE READ AND SIGN

---

few times, and it may no longer be accessible. As a result, they want you to recover the data and transfer it to another machine. A data recovery is not the same as a data transfer, so make sure to have separate listings for each.

2.4a What qualifies as a data transfer?

If the hard drive can be read, the data can be transferred easily to another computer. If this is the case, you can complete a data transfer. However, make sure the customer knows that when a hard drive is failing, even the transfer process itself could cause the hard drive to fail further. Therefore, this cannot be a guaranteed service. You can guarantee to attempt the transfer, but you cannot guarantee what will be recovered. Explaining this up front prevents problems down the line. To be clear, use a data transfer agreement like the one shown in Sample 3. Having the customer sign up front will help make it clear what can and can't be transferred.

CHECKLIST 3
WIPE AND RELOAD

Steps for Wipe and Reload	Completed
Find and record OS key: _____	
Install operating system	
Install all drivers	
Complete all OS updates	
Install antivirus program	
Install ancillary programs	

2.4b What qualifies as a data recovery?

If you have to complete any special work to recover the data, you are embarking on a data recovery. Like a data transfer, you cannot guarantee the results, so the customer is paying you to try to recover data, not based on the data you recover. Make sure that you are clear with the customer about the fact that you are not charging for the data that is recovered but for the attempt to recover the data. This is a very important distinction and if you are not clear about it up front, the customer may not agree to pay after the work is completed.

Also, be careful about attempting any type of recovery that will damage the hard driver further. If you do not have a "clean room" or the tools to complete a more aggressive data recovery, you don't want to damage the hard drive beyond repair. Know your limits!

One way to try to recover a drive is to freeze it for a short time. Just take the hard drive, put it into a static bag, then place it in a Ziploc bag and put it in the freezer for around two hours. When you take it out, place it immediately on the server and attempt to pull off the data. If it works, you will probably have at least 20 to 30 minutes to get the data off the drive! It will work 1 in 100 times, but when it does, you

will have a customer for life. This is a last-ditch effort by the way. Not for the faint of heart.

While many of us can work with hard drives to recover a good deal of data, there are some situations that most stores just aren't prepared for. If you need to actually take apart the drive in a clean room, you are probably not going to be able to handle that at your location. Instead, try partnering with another company that specializes in these services. One of the companies that we partner with is DriveSavers Data Recovery, a nationally recognized company that actually pays local computer stores referrals and gives the customers you refer a discount for services. With a range of custom services (including a photos-only option) and the ability to recover data even after fire, flood, deletion, and more, you can give your customers additional options for recovery.

It's important to note that recovery isn't always possible. If the drive fails while your system is trying to write a file, it's possible for the heads to actually touch the platters inside. If this happens, there is no recovery possible. The platters spin at more than 5400 RPM and sometimes up to 10K. I lost data through this and even though I was willing to pay, the company told me there was nothing it could do. My wife was *not* happy!

2.4c Validate the data recovery or data transfer

After you have completed a data recovery and/or transfer, and you believe you have a customer's data, make sure you validate the data with the person before wiping or recycling his or her hard drive. In some cases, *most* files are transferred but not all the files. Making sure the customer has what he or she wants *before* you do any other work will make it easier to resolve any problems. The easiest way to do this is to invite the customer to come in (or use remote tools) and look at the files that were recovered.

Note: When you are showing a customer a data recovery, there are times that you will come across family (or sometimes more colorful) photos, but *never* comment on any of these. Remember, in some households computers are used by multiple individuals and the person who brought in the computer may not be the primary user. Making comments on photos can only lead to uncomfortable conversations.

We have all heard horror stories about technicians who have poked around on a customer's computer and gotten caught. Don't let this happen in your business. Customer data is confidential and should remain confidential. While you may choose to keep a customer's data on your server after pickup (it is a good idea to keep a backup until the customer confirms that everything has been transferred) it is not a good idea to read the files, look at the photos, or scan the directories. In our company, it's an offense that means termination.

Sample 3 is an example of a Data Transfer Agreement.

3. Laptop Repairs

Today, more and more consumers are buying laptop systems. They can have all the features of a desktop with more portability. College students, businesspeople, and even children are starting to lean toward laptops. This means that your business will probably see quite a bit of laptop repair. The downside of laptop repair is that laptops are much harder to fix.

Let's say the problem is a software issue. If you have a tech bench, it is easy to hook up 8 to 16 desktops immediately to the system. The customer doesn't have to bring in anything except for the tower, and you can easily hook it up to your switch box to multitask. Unfortunately it isn't as easy with laptops.

Laptops all need their own power cord so always ask the customer to leave it with you. Even if you have a compatible charger, it is better to use the customer's power cord.

When you are taking apart a laptop you will need a lot of space to work on the computer. It isn't as easy to hook up into your switch box so you may choose to just leave it on top of your bench taking up almost as much space as two desktops! If you are waiting for specialized parts, you can either rebuild the system or you will need to obtain a large plastic bin to house the laptop and its parts.

When you are taking apart a laptop it may be tempting to leave it on your desk in its disassembled state. However, if you do this, you run the risk of losing parts — everything from screws to hard drives could be moved and lost for good. Always track the laptop parts

SAMPLE 3
DATA TRANSFER AGREEMENT

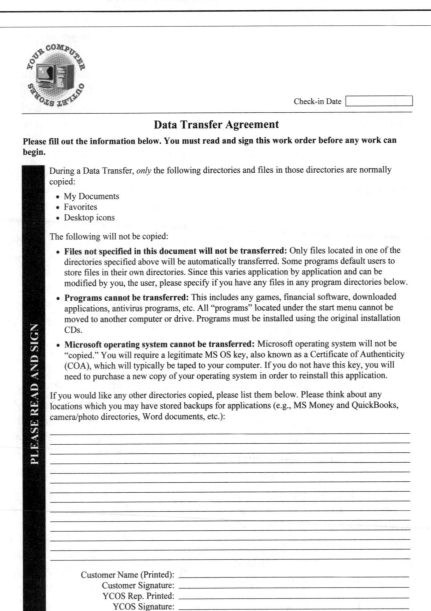

Check-in Date [   ]

Data Transfer Agreement

Please fill out the information below. You must read and sign this work order before any work can begin.

During a Data Transfer, *only* the following directories and files in those directories are normally copied:

- My Documents
- Favorites
- Desktop icons

The following will not be copied:

- **Files not specified in this document will not be transferred:** Only files located in one of the directories specified above will be automatically transferred. Some programs default users to store files in their own directories. Since this varies application by application and can be modified by you, the user, please specify if you have any files in any program directories below.

- **Programs cannot be transferred:** This includes any games, financial software, downloaded applications, antivirus programs, etc. All "programs" located under the start menu cannot be moved to another computer or drive. Programs must be installed using the original installation CDs.

- **Microsoft operating system cannot be transferred:** Microsoft operating system will not be "copied." You will require a legitimate MS OS key, also known as a Certificate of Authenticity (COA), which will typically be taped to your computer. If you do not have this key, you will need to purchase a new copy of your operating system in order to reinstall this application.

If you would like any other directories copied, please list them below. Please think about any locations which you may have stored backups for applications (e.g., MS Money and QuickBooks, camera/photo directories, Word documents, etc.):

_____
_____
_____
_____
_____
_____
_____
_____
_____
_____
_____

Customer Name (Printed): _____
Customer Signature: _____
YCOS Rep. Printed: _____
YCOS Signature: _____
Date: _____

(e.g., external drives, power cords) and label them with the customer's name as soon as it is checked in.

Now, let's say the laptop had a hardware problem. Laptop hardware repairs are somewhat more difficult than desktop hardware repairs. The best way to start a laptop repair is to look up the teardown instructions online and follow those. Laptop hardware takes more time to diagnose. Whereas desktop systems should take you no more than a few screws to pull apart, laptops can take a half hour, or sometimes more, just to get to the point where you can visually inspect the motherboard. It will then take another half hour to put the computer back together. This means that before you even start testing the parts, you have invested an hour or more in the diagnosis. Therefore, we recommend charging an hour of labor for hardware diagnosis.

Laptop parts are usually proprietary, meaning you can't easily swap one motherboard or graphics card for another. Instead, the parts usually need to be special-ordered for each system.

Keep these things in mind when you are pricing laptop work and estimating repairs. Because laptop repairs are a bit more customized, you will need to charge for this work differently than your desktop repairs. Even experienced technicians find that with the extensive variations in laptop designs, some work takes much longer than expected.

3.1 Ordering custom laptop parts

Once again, laptop repair is custom work. Even when you know what part is bad, you have to research a vendor, find the part, and order it online. Then, you need to manage the new vendor relationship and if the part fails, the customer will go to you for a replacement. Therefore, you need to charge for the new part. We recommend adding a 20 percent surcharge to any parts ordered with a minimum that is about the same as what you charge for 15 minutes of work. Since these are custom parts, we recommend instituting the following policies:

- **Customer must pay 100 percent of the part cost *up front* for a custom part order.** If you want, the customer can pay for service after the work is completed.

- **Custom orders are all final sale.** This means that a customer cannot return the part or change his or her mind on the work.

- **Custom work is not guaranteed to fix all the laptop problems.** This means that even if the replacement part doesn't fix all the issues, the customer still owes you for the work completed. For example, if a screen problem isn't identified because the computer didn't boot, you aren't responsible for fixing that problem for free.

We have had a few customers who have tried to get us to guarantee all the laptop parts when we replace just one. Replacing a motherboard doesn't guarantee that the wireless card, screen, or hard drive is still working. However, because of the costs of some custom parts, customers feel that you "owe" them more repairs because of the amount they spent. Make sure to explain your warranty policies and limitations before you complete any custom work or custom orders. To be clear, use a laptop hardware repair agreement like the one in Sample 4. This is an easy way to ensure your customers are aware of your policies.

Check-in Date ☐

Laptop Hardware Repair Agreement

Please fill out the information below. You must read and sign this work order before any work can begin.

PLEASE READ AND SIGN

Laptop repairs can often be time-consuming, difficult, and require proprietary parts for your specific machine. Therefore, Your Computer Outlet Stores (YCOS) requires that you understand the following about your laptop repair:

- **Laptop hardware repair will take a *minimum* of 4 business days to complete:** Laptop repair can be time-consuming and requires a large workspace. Therefore, laptop repair is not completed on-site. Your laptop will be transferred by courier to our laptop technicians (there is no cost for this courier service). If parts are available, your laptop may be fixed in four business days or less. However, since laptop parts are proprietary, parts may need to be ordered and, therefore, the laptop repair may take an additional five to seven business days, and in some cases, longer.

- **Proprietary parts will require payment in advance:** Since laptops often require propriety parts, special parts may need to be ordered specifically for your machine. If these parts are necessary, you will be contacted. You will be provided the cost of each component and will need to pay for the parts, plus shipping and handling at the time they are ordered. The costs for these parts are nonrefundable even if you later choose to forgo the laptop hardware repair.

- **Your Computer Outlet Stores (YCOS) is not responsible for lost or damaged files:** As with any computer repair it is possible, although rare, for a drive to fail mechanically during any repair. It is highly recommended that the customer back up any files prior to check-in.

Customer Name (Printed): _____
Customer Signature: _____
YCOS Rep. Printed: _____
YCOS Signature: _____
Date: _____

In general, we charge hourly labor on repairs with flat charges for certain services (e.g., keyboard and screen replacements). The result is that the cost of repairs tends to be much higher for laptops than for desktops.

3.2 Motherboard replacements

One common part that goes out on laptops is the motherboard. In many cases, what is a cost-effective repair on a desktop is a waste of money on a laptop. For instance, let's say that a customer brings in a laptop that is having motherboard issues. While this repair may be a reasonable option with a desktop, you will find that buying the replacement laptop motherboards at *your* cost can be hundreds of dollars. This means that once you add in labor (at least an hour, maybe two) plus the cost of a motherboard, handling fees, and shipping, the repair on a laptop motherboard could cost the customer between $300 and $400. What's more, after the repair is complete you may find other problems which hadn't been noticed beforehand (e.g., the wireless card isn't working).

In these cases, when the cost of the repair is close to the price of a new system, we highly discourage the repair both for our sake and the customer's. As a technician, charging a customer $400 for a service means the customer wants the service to be perfect. Unfortunately, this cannot be guaranteed with laptop repair. The replacement part could be defective and most replacement parts are refurbished ones that come with only a limited 30- to 60-day warranty. Other times, what broke the motherboard impacted other systems as well. Meaning after the work is done the computer still doesn't work and the customer doesn't want to pay for the work.

3.3 Power jack repairs

One of the most common parts that fail on a laptop motherboard is the connection between the power cord and the board — the jack. Because of rough handling, the pressure from the cord pushes the jack off the motherboard. The effect is that the power no longer reaches the board so the computer doesn't work. This is easy to diagnose since the jack is usually very loose. If you apply even slight pressure to the plug, it will move significantly from side to side.

Some local shops will agree to open the machine and solder the jack back down onto the motherboard for around $100. This is not very hard to do and usually fixes the problem. The issue is what happens next: Typically, soldering a part back onto a board does not guarantee the repair. This means that although the part has been secured to the board, rough handling (or sometimes even gentle handling) can make

it come off again. So, can you guarantee this work? Also, is this a "real" fix even if it doesn't have the same security as a new board? And lastly, is soldering a board risky?

In general, we don't recommend completing this work without a thorough explanation to the customer. Explain how this problem arises (customer handling) and explain that it could easily occur again. Make sure the customer understands that since this is a result of abuse, there is no guarantee on the work. It could happen again in a month or never. It is up to the customer, not up to the workmanship. Communication is the key to preventing customer conflict.

4. Research What Your Competitors Offer

A way to find out what services you should offer is to research your competition. First, look at local big-box stores that offer computer repairs. Companies such as Best Buy (Geek Squad) and Staples often have price lists that they can share that will provide a detailed listing of all their services and the price for those services. In general, the price at a big-box store should be your upward maximum. Don't try to price your services like these retailers; instead, figure out just how much your customers can save going to you instead of a large box store. This information may be a strong selling point during conversations with potential customers.

Next, visit any small, local computer stores in your area. Although they don't have the same information readily available (most will not have forms to give out to customers) they probably have some or most of their service prices prominently posted. Talk to the technicians, find out what services customers use most, and how long they take. These stores will be your biggest competition, so knowing their cost and turnaround time will help you understand what your customers will expect from you.

It may sound counterintuitive, but it is sometimes helpful to be friendly with the competition. You may find that although you are in the same area you do very different types of work. Although it doesn't happen often, sometimes you will find yourself referring your customers to another vendor and vice versa. In some cases, you can even build referral fees into this type of relationship!

5. Know Your Customers

As with any business, you have to know who your customers really are. Do you plan to target small-business owners? Seniors who don't want to mess with their computers? Young gamers who want high-end systems? In general, each of these groups has different needs and goals.

The benefit of knowing your customers is that it gives you the option of targeting your services. On one hand, if you are in the middle of a college town you probably won't find many students who want you to install software for them. Maybe some of the students would like this service, but the majority of college-aged people are capable of installing their own software. On the other hand, if you live by a retirement community, you may find that this service is one that is frequently requested. Older computer users may be comfortable with computers but often don't like making modifications to their own systems — even if it is only installing software.

Identifying what type of market is in your general area will also help you to design effective ads that get the attention of the customers you are looking for. In general, it would be better to have many custom ads, than one or two generic ads.

6. Determining Your Service Policy

As a computer repair business, you need to firmly establish your service policy. You need to ask yourself some questions about what you recommend for your customers.

What happens when your solution doesn't work? If a service is attempted but does not resolve the problem, is the customer responsible for the cost of the service? Do you charge the customer or not? Many stores do. As a matter of fact, most check-in paperwork will tell you that the customer is responsible for paying for all authorized work even if it doesn't resolve the problem. While this makes sense because you have invested time and effort into solving the problem, the customer may be a bit irritated if he or she is paying for a service that didn't help.

At our store, we indicate that we can charge our customers for services that are completed (even if they don't resolve the issue) but we generally don't. We have this listed on our paperwork to protect us from completing requested work that is beyond our control. For example, let's say we complete a data recovery that gets back 50 percent of the data, but not the specific photo the customer was looking for. In that case, we would charge the customer for the service because we completed the requested service to the best of our ability but we couldn't control what data was recovered and what was corrupted.

What if the service we recommended didn't work? Let's say a customer brings in a computer that has intermittent problems. After looking it over, you conclude that the operating system (OS) is corrupted and recommend that it be reloaded. He or she agrees to pay the $120 you charge for the service and you perform a wipe and reload for her. After the work is completed, you notice that the problems are still happening. You then run a detailed hard drive test and notice that the hard drive is going bad. What do you do? There are really only two choices:

1. Charge for the service you performed, even though it didn't resolve the problem; or

2. Don't charge for the service that didn't work.

That is the decision you will have to make. After all, the work was completed in good faith and, in most cases, this service would have fixed the problem. However, at our store, we would not charge the customer. Why? We choose to guarantee that a service will fix the problem or there is no charge. There are a few reasons why we think this works best:

- **Increases customer confidence:** Letting the customer know that your service either fixes the problem or it's free lets him or her know that you are confident in your diagnostic skills.

- **Most customers will agree to additional services even if they cost more:** When you call the customer to let him or her know that the service didn't work, he or she will usually be responsive to letting you try something else if the problem wasn't resolved. This means you will still be able to earn money for completing the repair even if it takes you a bit longer than you expected.

- **Diagnostics can be done faster.** If you aren't willing to work on a machine unless you are 100 percent certain that you know exactly what the problem is, you will find that you spend way more time on diagnostics than you need. For instance, if you suspect viruses, start a virus removal.

Now, let's say that you choose to guarantee your recommendation. You can call the customer and say that while you were working on the OS reload you noticed that the hard drive is also failing. If she wants to repair the computer it will be nearly $220; if she wants to scrap the computer, you can recycle it for her. At this point, she has a choice. Some of our customers do agree to do the additional work. Others choose to replace the computer and often will purchase a new machine from us and recycle the old one with us. I don't imagine they would do either if we told them we were going to charge them $119 for nothing.

Another question you will receive from customers is whether or not the computer is worth fixing. Unfortunately, there are never any hard and fast rules about this.

When the economy was booming, customers used almost any computer problem as a great excuse to buy a new computer. Have viruses, get a new computer! Bad hard drive, get a new computer! Need drivers, get a new computer! Well, almost. The truth is when customers have cash they sometimes just want to spend it. One customer sent her husband in with her old computer. When we diagnosed it we realized it was a good machine that could be dramatically improved with just a bit of memory. We added the RAM, and the woman came by to pick it up. She was furious. Apparently, she had sent her husband to our store to get a new computer. Even though her machine was now as fast as a new machine, she was still upset that he had "taken the cheap route"!

In a slow economy, the market is completely different. Customers are looking to spend the least amount of money possible. Almost anything is preferable than having to spend money on a new computer or even a refurbished system. We have had customers who wanted to replace the hard drive, reinstall the operating system, and even replace the motherboard on an old computer because the total was less than a new machine — even though for a little bit more money they would have had a much better system!

Our perspective on fixing computers is to give the customer the best options available. However, not all computer stores adhere to this philosophy. On the one hand, a new computer for $400 usually has a low margin, maybe about $80. On the other hand, completing software repairs on an old computer could run up to $300 and that money would be all margin. Therefore, you will find some businesses that recommend a customer make an expensive repair in place of spending a few dollars more and getting a better value. While this is not illegal, businesses that do behave like this will eventually build a reputation of recommending unnecessary services.

The best thing to do is to give the customer all the information and make a recommendation that is not based on what makes you the most money, but what is best for the customer. In the end, this will not just benefit the customer but also help build your business with customers that trust you. In addition, we've found that many times customers have gone to one of the big-box stores before they came to us. They were told they needed an $800 system and when we told them we could fix their problem for less than $200, they were overjoyed. They told everyone and we got more happy customers!

7

Pricing Your Services

nce you know what services you want to offer to your targeted customers, you need to get an idea of what it will cost for you to provide these services.

1. Calculating What Your Time Costs

You may have started your business in your garage (a starting place shared by many successful companies) to reduce your overhead. Your first customer calls and you decide you're going to charge $49 for one hour of labor. How much money will you make? It is tempting to say $49; after all, that is your gross profit, but in truth, your actual profit takes into account all the other money you are spending for the month. The question becomes, "Can I be profitable at $49 per hour? If I get enough customers, what is the maximum amount I can make at this price?"

Fortunately, there is an easy way to answer these questions. The easiest way to calculate this is to total all your business expenses and then divide that by the number of paid hours you expect to work. See Sample 5.

From this sample, you can see that if your expenses are up at $2,000 per month (which is very high for a small business without a retail location), the cost of doing business each hour is $11.63. This means that if you have customers paying you $49 per hour, your profit will be about $37.37 per hour or approximately $6,400 per month after expenses!

This also tells you how much you can lower your price to still be competitive. Obviously, any service that costs only $20 per hour will be priced too low as this will leave you around minimum wage for your hard work! Use Worksheet 1 (also included on the CD) to determine what your expenses are per hour and from there you will understand your pricing minimums.

SAMPLE 5
EXPENSES PER HOUR

Expenses per month = $2,000
Hours per month = (40 hours per week) x (4.3 weeks per month)
Hours per month = 172
Total expenses per hour = Expenses per month/Hours worked per month
Total expenses per month = $2,000/172 = $11.63

WORKSHEET 1
EXPENSES PER HOUR

Expenses	Cost per Month
Rent	
Utilities (include phone, cable, Internet, etc.)	
Insurance	
Licenses	
Subscriptions (include LogMeIn, MS Action Pack)	
Office supplies (include copy paper, printer ink, CDs, etc.)	
Bank fees (including credit card processing, etc.)	
Total Expenses per Month	

Hours per month = (hours/week) x (4⅓ weeks per month)	
Total expenses per hour = Expenses per month/Hours worked per month	
Total expenses per month	$
Total expenses per hour	$

2. Calculating Flat-Rate Services

In computer repair, calculating flat-rate services is one of the harder measurements to accomplish. Let's say that you are "working" on a virus removal. You may spend a half hour at first getting around the viruses, installing scanning tools, etc., but after that, you may no longer be staring at the computer. Instead you will have kicked off scans that run for hours with no interference from you. However, you have to be on-site to watch the systems and make sure that the next tool is started on time. So, if the computer takes two to three days to complete all these scans, how much time did you actually spend? How much time should you charge the customer or, in other words, how do you price the service?

SAMPLE 6
COMPUTER BUSINESS SERVICES FLAT RATES

Service	Description	Estimated Time	Cost
Tune-up	Complete some regular maintenance functions, including defrag, stopping unnecessary services, etc.	1 hour	$49
Virus removal	Computers are scanned with three to four virus removal tools over the course of three to four days.	3 hours	$149
Wipe and reload	Complete reinstallation of the OS, including updates to all drivers.	2.5 hours	$129

One you know who your customers are and what your competitors are offering and for how much, you are ready to create your service list. To do this you need to define the following:

- What is the service you are offering?

- What is the description of the service? (Make sure to think about what work this includes and does not include.)

- How much of your time will it take to complete the work?

- How much is the charge?

Some examples of services that your business can provide with some sample pricing are listed in Sample 6.

Once you have that complete, you may want to make an abbreviated version for your desk or office. For this version, you can eliminate the description and time estimate (which can vary based on the actual computer and could be misleading if any customer saw it) and just keep it simple. See Sample 7.

3. Estimating Custom Work

If you are completing a service or a type of service that you haven't priced before, try to keep the work in line with your other prices. In general, let the customer know the expected price up front and give yourself some room for error. For example, if the service you want to offer will take you three hours or so of straight work, you may price it around $159; but if you think that there may be more custom work involved, you may let the customer know that the bill can be as high as $199 to give yourself some wiggle room.

4. Check Your Pricing

Once you estimate your prices, you still need to determine if your prices are reasonable for your market. There are a few factors that go into competitive pricing:

- **Retail versus home-based business:** In general, you can charge more if you work out of a retail storefront than if you are working out of your home (because the overhead is lower, people expect to pay less). If your prices are the same as a local computer store, they are probably too high.

- **Compare your pricing to big-box stores:** Your pricing should let your customers know that you are providing significant savings over the big-box stores (you may even want to put this in your ad). Your prices should be at least 20 to 30 percent less; in some cases, you may want to reduce your prices even further compared to the big-box stores.

- **Compare your prices to others in your advertising space:** Another place to check your pricing is where you plan to advertise. If everyone else in that market is either much higher or much lower, your prices may need to be adjusted.

You may also want to add an hourly rate. This will allow you to expand to services you haven't anticipated. As you work with your customers you may find that they have problems that you can solve, but it is not a service on the list. For these items you can simply estimate the amount of time the work will take and charge by the half hour with a half hour minimum. For instance, when we first started, we had a few people that came in asking for driver updates. At first, we completed this service as a half-hour labor. Eventually, we listed it as a separate service. See Sample 7.

SAMPLE 7
COMMON IN-STORE SERVICES

#	Service Description	Price
Common In-Store Services		
	FREE 15-minute in-store diagnostic	FREE
3494	Minimum service charge (unlisted services)	$24.50
982	1-hour in-store labor	$49
1745	Extended diagnostic	$49
941	Tune-up	$49
946	Wipe and reload	$119
944	Windows repair	$119
1049	Winsock fix	$49
3127	Wipe and reload with data transfer	$159
1025	Quick scan virus removal	$89
1047	Detailed virus and spyware removal	$189
2099	Full data transfer — from one machine to another	$69
3495	Limited data transfer — transfer up to 1 CD of files	$29
1252	Data recovery — recover data from a failed hard drive	$159
3500	Hard drive sector repair	$69
985	Basic software installation	$20
1052	Complex software installation	$49
	McAfee installation with the purchase of McAfee	FREE
3496	Driver updates — resolve up to 5 problem drivers	$30
1006	Ghosting	$69
1050	Wireless setup	$49

#	Service Description	Price
Part Installation		
3497	Part installation — sold by *(insert your business name)*	$15
3498	Part installation — purchased at another vendor	$25
3499	Part installation — Transfer from a customer computer to a computer being purchased at *(insert your business name)*	$15

#	Item Description	Price
Laptop Repair		
3243	Laptop hourly repair	$69
	Jack repair — estimate — $99 (No warranty on length of repair as it depends on customer's care)	
3353	Laptop jack repair service	$99
	Jack repair part estimate*	$10
	Keyboard — estimate — $59	
3352	Laptop keyboard replacement service	$29
	Keyboard part estimate*	$30
	Screen — estimate — $139	
3351	Laptop screen replacement service	$39
	Screen part estimate*	$100
	Motherboard — estimate — $269	
3350	Laptop motherboard replacement service	$69
	Motherboard part estimate*	$200
	Fan — estimate — $89	
3361	Laptop fan replacement service	$69
	Fan part estimate*	$20
	Video card — estimate — $109	
3378	Laptop video card replacement service	$69
	Video part estimate*	$40
	Power button — estimate — $79	
3384	Laptop power button replacement service	$39
	Power button part estimate*	$40
	WiFi card — estimate — $89 (It is usually less expensive and better to install a new wireless card.)	
3354	Laptop WiFi card replacement service	$39
	WiFi part estimate*	$50
*Note: Part estimates are only a ballpark of the estimated cost — laptop model, manufacturer, part availability, and shipping costs will cause the actual price to vary. Before any repair is completed, an estimate for the customer's particular computer will be provided.		

Diagnosing
a Computer

When a customer presents you with a computer, it is tempting to just get right down to business. Many people start by finding out about the problem, opening up the computer, and trying to solve the problem. However, this approach could put your business at risk, cost you a sale, or just cause more confusion than it solves.

Whenever you do any work on a computer, you should always start by using a standard diagnostic process. Even if your customer is not going to leave the computer with you, you should always track the work on the customer's check-in form. While this may sound time-consuming, it will actually save you a great deal of time and effort (and sometimes money). The check-in form can serve many different purposes:

- The customer receives a copy of the form and this serves as his or her check-in receipt as well as gives him or her your contact information.

- Collects customer information so that you can contact him or her when the work is done or if you have additional questions.

- Your policies are clearly outlined to the customer.

- The customer's problem is documented.

- The customer's approval is documented.

- The work you complete is documented.

- The customer signs the form at the end of the work to show he or she has accepted the work that was performed.

At our store we also use the blank back of forms like these for detailed notes about the computer. Everything from the problems we encountered during the diagnostic to our interaction with our customers is recorded on the back of the form. During the check-in process, the form is taped to the computer. After work is completed, the form is saved and filed in case any future problems arise.

1. Designing Your Check-in Form

The forms we use were actually developed over the years to meet the needs of our technicians. They have changed over time, and yours will too. Every time we reorder our forms from the printer, we ask our technicians if they need any changes to the form first — many times they do have suggestions that improve the form.

Therefore, use Sample 8 (also included on the CD as "Check-in Form") as a starting point. As you work with it, feel free to customize it as needed to meet the needs of your business. Because the check-in form contains so much critical information, it will become the most important form in your business so make sure you take the time to ensure that the form meets your needs. The following outlines what should go into the check-in form.

Check-in summary (across the top): One thing that we like to put on our forms is a blank line where we boldly write the customer name and check-in date. This lets us track our check-ins.

Store information (across the top): Across the top we list our store information, including logo, address, and phone number. Even though the customer has left his or her computer with us, we found that he or she still may not know where we are located or how to contact us. We add this information to the top of the form so that the customer has this information after the check-in is completed.

This is also a good place to locate a welcome message to your customers. We also add instructions for the form at the top although we walk each customer through the form personally.

Customer information (top left): This section contains the information that you need to have about the customers (e.g., name, address, and phone number). If they forget to fill in a phone number, you will be unable to contact them when the work is complete. We had one customer who did this and came in furious about a month later. While it was her fault for skipping this information on the form and not calling for an update, it didn't stop her from yelling at us!

We also ask for the customer to indicate if this is a business or consumer machine. This is an important talking point for you. If it is a business computer, you may need to get other information. For instance, is the problem happening on or off their network? Is this critical to have fixed before a particular date (e.g., a payroll computer)? Does the customer want a data backup before any work is completed (we usually charge for this service)?

Lastly, what is the password on the machine? There is nothing worse than having to wait to get the password or, if you can't get a hold of the customer, having to break the password. Either way, it wastes *your* time, so get this information up front.

Computer check-in information (top right): When you collect a customer's computer, sometimes the person has other things with the machine. For example, a laptop may also have a case, an external CD drive, etc. Do *not* let the customer check in these items! As a technician, you don't need the case, or anything in the case. All this will do is clutter your work area and give you things to lose. The things that get checked in should be listed on the form.

Company policy information (middle): This is where you show your critical company policies. Make sure to list any disclaimers or other notifications you want to make sure each customer is aware of. Also, include a line where the customer can sign and date the policy. This will protect you in case of any problems in the future.

Make sure to keep the check-in forms as long as possible. When the customers sign the policy information, they are agreeing to the risks associated with computer repair. Therefore, *keep these forms* even after the repair is done. If there is any problem, this form will show that the customers knew the risks and accepted the risks. Their signature can save you hundreds if not thousands of dollars in lawsuits. They wouldn't have brought in the computer if there wasn't something wrong with it, but they tend to forget that when something bad happens. As an example, a virus removal will stress a hard drive far beyond what it commonly experiences. With the new power-saving drives, the number of hours they actually spin has been drastically reduced. When we do a virus removal the drive works at 100 percent capacity for 12 hours or more. They can fail so before we start, we tell that to customers to ensure they've backed up their data.

After a few years when you are ready to get rid of the forms, don't just throw them out, scan them in! There are some great scanners on the market (e.g., NeatReceipts) that can scan your forms and turn them into searchable PDF documents. While the search feature may not always work on handwritten text, storing the forms electronically will let you have the reports for tax purposes or legal reasons without taking too much space in your home or business.

High-level tech notes (bottom left): This is where we put the high-level tech notes (remember we also keep more detailed notes on the back of the page). Make this area fit your business and contain information that is important to you.

Sign-offs (bottom right): At the end of the repair, you want to make sure that both you *and* the customer have tested the system. Use this area to track both of those functions.

In general, there are a few things that we realized we didn't need on the form. For instance, the form is not numbered. This is because we (unlike a Laundromat) use the form itself as the "ticket," not the number. Since the customer has filled out so much unique information, there is no need for a unique number. (Plus the cost of numbered forms is higher; don't get it if it doesn't add value).

Another thing we don't have is custom highlighting or color logos. The cost of adding additional colors to the form can almost double the printing costs. Try to keep your form in black and white. If your business is doing well, you could go through thousands of these forms each year, and every penny counts!

2. How to Complete a Diagnostic and Make a Sale

It may seem obvious, but it is important to use the check-in form the right way. If you skip any of the following steps, or if you fail to complete them in their entirety, you will find that additional problems will happen. Using the form helps you correctly diagnose your problem, build a customer relationship, and, most importantly, make a sale!

SAMPLE 8
CHECK-IN FORM

1 Hard Drive, Suite 404
Emmes, DOS DEDX9
(400) 500-1024

Check-in Date

Welcome to YOUR COMPUTER OUTLET STORES
You must fill out, read, and sign this work order before any work can begin.

	List ALL check-in items (computer, external drives, etc.)	Check-In Verification		Pick-Up Verification	
	Please initial:	Cust.	YCOS	Cust.	YCOS

PLEASE FILL OUT

Customer name:

Customer address:

Customer phone:

Alternate phone:

Is this a business computer?   Yes   No

Business name:

Computer password (if applicable):

Problem/Work request:

PLEASE READ AND SIGN

NO WORK WILL BE DONE ON ANY SYSTEM UNTIL WORK ORDER IS AGREED TO AND SIGNED.

Your Computer Outlet Stores (YCOS) is not responsible for lost or damaged files. *It is the customer's responsibility to back up any files on the computer prior to check in.* If you (the customer) are unable to save your files due to the condition of your computer, we will attempt to save the files for you, but YCOS is not responsible for any lost or damaged files.

NOTE: Any temporary internet files, temporary files, cookies, and recycle bin items **WILL BE REMOVED** during most services. YCOS is not responsible for any damages that may result from an attempt to repair an already damaged computer.

The first 15 minutes of the diagnostic is free. Our skilled technicians can usually give you the assessment in under 15 minutes. If you decide to proceed with repair, general labor will be charged from the time we start working on your system. Labor rate is $49.00 each hour, and we charge by the half hour (with the exception of fixed-rate services). YCOS will attempt to repair or upgrade your computer upon your request, but if the repair or upgrade is impossible due to unforeseen complications and/or other damage, you (the customer) will still be responsible for all labor charges incurred.

If your system/equipment is left at an YCOS location for more than 30 days, storage fee of $5/day will be assigned to your bill. After 60 days, YCOS will sell system/equipment to recover repair/storage fees. This is a rapid repair and sales facility; please respect our need to keep our shelves free of clutter.

If anyone else will be picking up the computer besides you (the customer), you must notify one of the YCOS employees. YCOS will not release the computer to anyone unless we have permission to do so.

Authorized Person: _____

I (customer) understand all of the above and I hereby release Your Computer Outlet Stores (YCOS) from all liability in repairing and/or upgrading my computer.

Customer Signature: _____   **Date:** _____

Problem diagnostic: Tech Init: _____	Quality Check	Tech	Mgr	Quality Check	Tech	Mgr
	NIC: surfs net			Drivers		
	Wireless connects			Antivirus		
Authorization to proceed: Yes No	Sound: plays sound			Front/back USB		
Verified: In person By phone	Optical drive reads			Cards screwed down		
Date and time:	Eject CD			Blown out and clean		
Labor tasks completed: Tech Init: _____	**Responsible technician:**			**Manager verification:**		
	Date(s) called for pick-up:					
New hardware installed: Tech Init: _____	**ACCEPTANCE OF WORK PERFORMED**					

ACCEPTANCE OF WORK PERFORMED
I acknowledge satisfactory completion of the described work and I acknowledge that I have picked up all of my checked-in items. I understand that I have had the opportunity to review the work at Your Computer Outlet Stores with a technician. Further, I understand that any issues that I think may be related to this service must be identified within 24 hours and the computer must be returned to YCOS within that 24-hour period for a technician to review.

Customer Signature: _____

2.1 Step 1: Ask the customer to complete the form

First and foremost have your customer complete your check-in form. This should include providing information about who the customer is. Specifically make sure to understand who uses the system. Is this a business system with a critical function or is it a computer used by a three-year-old? Knowing who the user is and what the machine is used for not only helps you make your diagnosis, but if there is a critical function that the computer has, you will know if you need to offer expedited service for an additional fee. Normally, expedited service would be completed ASAP, working nights and weekends to get the job done.

2.2 Step 2: Read the customer your policies

Policies are there for the customers to read, but give them a brief verbal overview of what your policies are and why you have them. This might take a minute or two, but it is worth it. After all, many people sign documents without ever reading them. Sure, they are supposed to read the document, but reading it to them makes sure they have the chance to ask any questions and makes sure you can emphasize any concerns.

2.3 Step 3: Have the customer sign the disclaimer

Every computer repair has risks. Even if the only risk is that your place of business is wiped away by a storm, things can happen. Getting the customers to sign off on the disclaimer makes them aware of and accepting of the risks involved. This also gives you the chance to discuss the risks of any type of work. For instance, if the hard drive is starting to fail,

this would be a good time to explain that hard drives can fail at any time — even while you are trying to do a data transfer. Setting these expectations up front reduces the problems you will have later on if there are any issues.

2.4 Step 4: Have the customer explain the problem

Even though the customers wrote the issues on the form, take the time to listen to what is wrong. Ask questions, and show that you are interested in their situation. At this point, you are showing the customers that you care about their individual situation and that you understand what they are saying. This is not just important to help speed along your diagnosis, but it will also help build your relationship with the customer.

By the way, some customers will lie. If they dropped their Notebook, it might not come out until much later. If they poured a soda into their computer, they will only admit it when you point to the pools of dried soda. If their computer is riddled with porn and pop-ups, they blame their neighbor. While it's useful to get information from the customers, you might have to treat them as "hostile witnesses"!

2.5 Step 5: Reproduce the problem

Once you understand the problem, it is important to reproduce it yourself. In some cases, your customers will be adamant that they know what is wrong and they don't want you to "waste" time checking it. To handle these customers, let them know that you need to see the error yourself to see what else is happening while the error occurs. Take notes as you work because you will want them later.

Always start your inspection of the computer by turning it on. This step may seem silly, especially if the customer says the computer won't even turn on, but you will be surprised at your results. In some cases, the computer the person claims isn't working will actually turn on (what the customer meant was that the computer won't boot). In other cases, people will claim computers work when they don't even turn on! Either way, it is best to check this point yourself.

2.6 Step 6: Identify the cause of the problem but do *not* fix it

Once you think you know the cause of the problem, stop: Do *not* fix the problem! Even if the problem is a small setting that you need to change, *never* fix the problem before speaking with the customer and getting approval to make the repair! This is a common mistake new techs make. Because the problem is a quick fix, they fix the problem first and then try to charge the customer later. However, this can create conflict.

We have had customers come in with all sorts of odd problems. Occasionally, the problem is something simple such as a small setting that needs to be changed. Unfortunately, if you change this setting first and then tell the customer he or she will be charged the minimum (i.e., a half hour of labor), the person will generally be upset and feel cheated. The problem is that when you fix it without mentioning the charge, the customer assumes it is free and he or she is disappointed and upset that there is a cost. However, if the person comes in with the problem and you tell him or her that you think you can fix it but he or she will be charged for a half hour of labor, the customer now has a choice. In general, most people choose the repair and they are thrilled that it didn't cost more.

Don't assume that the only problem the computer has is the problem the customer reported. We have seen customers check in computers for one problem and then we found a few other problems that weren't mentioned. Always give the computer a thorough once-over when you are checking it in. If you find any other problems, bring these to the attention of the customer right away so that he or she understands the problems were there *before* the repair was completed. Remember, if you replace the customer's power supply and three weeks later the person's hard drive dies, he or she will blame you for not knowing it was going to fail. Check everything you can as long as you have time and space.

2.7 Step 7: Obtain customer approval to complete the work

To obtain customer approval, you want the customer to understand three basic things:

1. **What is wrong and how much it will cost to fix?** Once you know the problem, tell the customer in general terms (not with such specificity that he or she could do it at home, just the high-level problem statement) what you think the issue is, how you think it can be resolved, and how much it will cost to resolve the problem. Then, ask for customer's approval to fix the problem. If the person doesn't approve, you simply put the machine back together and let him or her walk out with just the diagnostic completed.

2. **What can go wrong?** If the customer approves the repair, you can get started. Make sure he or she understands the risks of the particular service. Let the

customer know what could go wrong. Were the power supply *and* motherboard damaged? Make sure he or she knows that other parts could be broken as well. Is the computer blue-screening? Talk to the person about all the things that could cause that problem. By giving the customer information before the problem occurs you will prepare him or her for what could go wrong, making the conversation much easier when or if a problem happens.

3. **Approximately when will it be completed?** Let the customer know when you will be starting work on his or her system and about when you think work will be completed. If the customer brought in the computer on a Friday and you are closed until Monday, then let the person know that. This way, he or she isn't waiting all weekend expecting your call.

> Promised dates are always missed. I don't know why this is, but it often seems like any time a date is "promised," the delivery date is missed — every time. Therefore, never promise an exact date. You can give an estimated completion and you can promise to call by a particular time with an update, but avoid promising any repair by any particular date.

2.8 Step 8: Complete the work and check the computer

Although this is a short step, it can be the most difficult step. Once you think you have fixed the problem, make sure to check all the other computer functions to make sure that nothing else was broken in the process. We have a checklist that each tech is required to complete before the system is deemed finished. You'd

be surprised how many times a DVD cable is knocked off by accident when we're working inside a case, or we had to disconnect the USB ports and didn't plug them back in. When the customer gets home after carrying the heavy computer all the way back, he or she doesn't want to have to bring it back. We're trying to create happy customers, remember?

2.9 Step 9: Have the customer verify that the work is complete

Before the customer leaves your shop or before you leave the client site, make sure that the customer verifies that the computer is working. This step may take a couple of minutes, but it builds strong customer relationships and makes any problems found in the next few days easier to understand. For instance, one customer picked up a computer and verified it worked. When he got home and plugged it in, it didn't even turn on. Had he not verified it at our store, he would have been convinced we gave him an unfixed computer. However, when he called, he started by apologizing for "breaking it" before he got it home and mentioned that he had to drive on a long unpaved road to get to his house. He brought back the machine, we fixed it again (for free as a courtesy — the hard drive cable had just "bounced out"), and he was happy. Had he not verified the machine was working before he left, it would have been a very different phone conversation.

Note: You have a customer that says he or she wants to save money on service. The person offers to pay you half the rate, but in exchange, he or she will do part of the service himself or herself. Never, ever take this deal. Each time we have tried working with customers like these they are more trouble and time than having a customer who gets the full service. For example, one customer offered to install his own drivers, and do his own updates on a wipe and reload only to go home and complain that "nothing worked" when he got there! It is not worth your time to negotiate partial service.

2.10 Step 10: Collect your payment

Once the work is complete, collect any payment you are due before the computer leaves your shop or before you leave the client site.

Choosing
Your Stock

Although many technicians will tell you they hate selling, computer business owners love sales. Selling merchandise is often more profitable than selling service. For instance, if a customer completes a service with our business, the customer generally pays at a rate of $13 for 15 minutes of service. However, if the same customer purchases a few items, the sale can take only 15 minutes, but it could generate hundreds of dollars in profit. Therefore, every computer business should focus on having the products customers need and want.

The stock a store carries can vary from business to business depending on the customer base. Our store is geared toward customers looking for a bargain. We stock refurbished computers, affordable parts, and specialize in providing *free* diagnostics. However, just a few blocks from one of our stores is another small computer business retailer that specializes in gaming computers. That store sells high-end computers (a much smaller and more difficult market) and as a result, the store is stocked with large screen TVs, high-end monitors, and the latest graphic cards. Both types of stores have the right stock for their customer base, although there is a great deal of difference between the two. Therefore, as you read this chapter, think about your particular target market.

1. What Type of Stock Do You Need?

When we purchased our first computer store it was full of stock. The previous owners sold everything from CD cases that looked like stuffed animals to audio component cables and computer games. Five years later, we still have much of that original inventory. What's worse is that we found that having a crowded store meant we had difficulty managing our inventory and our customers had a hard time knowing what we sold! Once someone even asked us if we sold computers! When we opened our second store, we sold hardly anything. The shelves had only our best-selling products and our entire investment was around $5,000. So, which is right?

Well, it depends on what type of store you want to be. In our case we decided to reduce our inventory to computer-related items only. When you are starting out, it is best to limit your inventory to items you know you can sell. Otherwise, you could wind up with lots of furry CD cases!

The items that we discovered are big sellers include:

- New desktops and laptops

- Refurbished desktops and laptops

- Monitors

- Product warranties (these can be third-party)

- Hard drives (laptop and desktop)

- RAM (DDR, DDR2, and DDR3 for desktops and notebooks)

- Optical drives (CD, DVD, Blu-ray drives)

- Printers and printer ink

- Peripherals such as wireless keyboards, mice, speakers, etc.

- Sound adapters (these use a USB slot to add audio)

- External hard drives and hard drive cases

- Virus protection

- Microsoft software including operating systems and MS Office

- USB flash drives

- Universal laptop AC adapters

- Backup power supply with voltage regulators

- Surge protectors and power strips

- Routers and network cards

- Graphic cards (we usually keep the most recent technology cards as well as one or two older models for repairs)

- Cables (Cat 5, HDMI, etc.)

2. Parts You Probably Shouldn't Stock

As you are building your inventory it will be tempting to stock parts that are specifically focused on potential business clients. Items like RAID cards, server parts, oversized monitors, etc., are all tempting items to carry. However, you should keep these items as special order. After all, if a business client does need these items, you can always get them quickly (even if you have to buy them retail) but you can't always return them to your vendor if you don't sell them quickly.

Never buy more stock than you need for a month or so. Prices on parts change fast and new technology is constantly being released. Even if you are getting a great deal, it may not be worth buying too much of a product unless you are sure you can move it quickly. The last thing you want to do is be stuck with thousands of dollars of outdated parts!

3. Carrying New Computers

If you are going to sell new desktop computers, the most cost-effective way to do this is to build them yourself. Choosing the parts you use, the manufacturers, and the specs allows you to build systems that your customers will love, that will be profitable, and that won't have many warranty claims.

When you start carrying computers, choose only a couple — maybe three — different price points. While this sounds limiting, it allows you to offer your customers a choice without creating mayhem. Offering too many models will cause confusion, increase your costs to stock inventory, and will sometimes hinder your sales.

At our store, we regularly carry only three desktop models and we describe them by price (since the specs change based on the market). During the economic boom, we sold computers for $899, $599, and $399. During the bust we sold computers for $599, $499, and $399. Although we can upgrade the $599 to become any type of custom system, we rarely do.

Laptops are more difficult to manage. In general, you will need to get your laptops directly from a wholesaler. Unfortunately, the prices at wholesalers are nearly the same as prices at outlet stores and online retailers. Further, if you don't sell the laptops quickly, you will find that they become "old" technology quickly and, in a matter of months, they can be worth less than you paid. As a result, it is hard to be competitively priced and profitable with laptops. During the boom, we were able to sell laptops since the ancillary sales (e.g., warranties, laptop cases, mice) more than made up for the low margin on the computer. However, in today's market where people buy fewer add-ons, we usually don't offer new laptops for sale.

Check the prices and check the competition in your area. If you aren't sure, you can always buy one laptop and see how quickly it sells.

4. Carrying Notebook Parts

There are only three parts of the Notebook that you want to keep in stock:

- Hard drives (keep about three sizes of SATA and maybe one or two IDE).

- RAM (a few sticks of older DDR and DDR2 RAM as well as newer RAM such as DDR3).

- Universal power cords (this is an unusual product because you can buy it in bulk since you can sell this same model for six months or more).

Some places stock other Notebook parts, such as custom batteries or custom power cords, but unless you have a very large customer base, this type of inventory is difficult to move.

Other more custom parts (e.g., motherboards, wireless cards) are almost never purchased in advance. Even large online sellers don't usually buy these parts new. Most are recycled from older machines. Therefore, you can build an inventory. Every time a customer gives a laptop for you to recycle you can use this machine for parts, but make sure each component is thoroughly tested before it is sold. Other than that, you shouldn't expect to carry proprietary Notebook parts.

5. Finding Used Computer Equipment

One of our biggest sellers in any market is refurbished desktops, laptops, and monitors. During a boom, customers buy these systems as "kid-friendly" computers that they don't have to worry about (we once had a customer come in and buy one for each child). During a bust, customers buy these computers for themselves as an inexpensive way to get the technology they need to surf the Internet, create résumés, and get their work done. Either way, the low-end computers (less than $200) and refurbished monitors (less than $80) are popular selling items — if you can find a reliable vendor who sells them.

Vendors

There are many types of businesses at which you buy products from a few large vendors and payments and credits are easily handled. However, with computer repair and retail, you may find yourself working with other small businesses to purchase products such as used computers and outsourced repairs. Therefore, how you pay for things often becomes as important as where you buy them.

One of the worst things that can happen to a business's profitability is theft. It wastes your money, causes you unnecessary stress and problems, and makes it more difficult to meet your commitments. It is even worse when this theft happens from business partners. Unfortunately, not every business partner is scrupulous.

There are a few ways that you can research new business partners:

- **Better Business Bureau**: One thing that the BBB gives you is information about a company's complaint status. Not all reputable companies have an A rating. Sometimes, businesses may have complaints that they aren't aware of. If you think the business you want to work with is in this category, let them know about the outstanding issues and see if they can resolve them and improve their rating.

- **References:** Some companies constantly burn bridges. Asking for references gives you a chance to speak with some recent customers. What is amazing is that not all references will be positive. Many people are candid when they are providing references and you may learn more than you would expect.

- **Internet references:** Another place to look for vendor feedback is on the Internet. To find reviews, just type the vendor's name in Google with the word "review" or "feedback" or "complaints." These searches will usually help you find information about the companies that you are thinking about working with.

Unfortunately, even companies you have done business with in the past can have problems in the future. Rarely will they let you know they are in trouble. For years, we ordered our check-in forms from the same company. They were a small shop that provided low prices even if they did take a little longer to deliver the forms we ordered. During our last reorder the owner asked us to pay by check instead of our usual credit card payment. We had talked a few times and it seemed reasonable. Credit cards can be expensive for the vendor (taking up to 5 percent of a sale) and our order was around $500. Since we had been ordering from them for years, we sent them a check. At first it seemed fine. They gave us an estimated delivery date and the check cleared. After that, the relationship soured. First, there were delays, excuses, and problems. Finally, they stopped taking our calls and didn't even pretend we were getting the product anymore. When we looked them up on the BBB their rating had dropped dramatically and they now held an "F" rating. We never got our forms and just wrote it off as a bad debt.

1. Finding Vendors

Finding vendors used to be one of the more difficult parts of running a small business. You needed to apply to the vendor, get credit lines, etc. However, with the advent of the Internet, there are many large retailers that offer pricing at or near wholesale. Sometimes their deal prices are so low and oftentimes coupled with free shipping so that they often meet or beat our wholesaler pricing on routers, monitors, operating system disks, etc. Some retailers for you to check out include club stores (e.g., Sam's Club and Costco) as well as Internet technology resellers (e.g., Newegg and Overstock).

Other retailers may seem like a good deal, but they are often not. Avoid products for resale at dollar stores (the quality is too low and sometimes the price is too high), Wal-Mart (your customers probably already shop there and may notice), and large office supply stores that often sell their custom brands for less.

If you are looking for custom parts, one of the best places to start your search is eBay. Just be sure to check the following before bidding:

- **Figure out the *final* price after shipping:** Sometimes shipping costs more than you think.

- **Check the "ship from" location:** Some parts are shipped from overseas and will take weeks to arrive.

- **Check the seller's reputation:** If the seller hasn't sold a lot of parts, or if it isn't highly rated, avoid it. Some people sell "untested" parts as tested and then just offer a return policy. Dealing with vendors like these can become time-consuming and frustrating for you and your customers.

- **Read the warranty information:** Do they accept returns? What amount of time? Your customers will expect at least a 30-day warranty, so look for a solid warranty from your vendor.

1.1 Industry wholesalers

There are many wholesalers in the computer industry and their prices vary. As mentioned before, sometimes, even online retailers can beat wholesalers' prices these days. However, if you want to check out a few large wholesalers, you may want to try the following companies:

- **Ma Labs (www.malabs.com):** To see pricing you will need to get a login and an assigned salesperson. Ma Labs carries most computer parts.

- **Tech Data (www.techdata.com):** Another parts supplier.

- **Printer Essentials (www. printeressentials.com):** This is an ink wholesaler in case you choose to carry printer ink as part of your offerings.

There are other local wholesalers that may specialize in used computers. One way to find these vendors is to join wholesaling networks. These networks can help you get in touch with companies in your area, which will reduce your shipping costs dramatically.

Note that the least expensive place to get used Notebooks is through a local wholesaler. Usually these individuals have relationships with large corporations and buy the computers in bulk. They then go through the machines, fix them, and resell them, this time with loaded, clean operating systems and warranties. Finding these resellers may be as easy as looking on Craigslist or a local directory.

1.2 Vendor terms

When a company offers you terms, it means that you can purchase its products and services and then have a period of time (the term) in which to pay it back. Usually, the term is about 30 days, but sometimes, it can be 60 or even 90. The benefit of terms is obvious; you can stock your store and pay for your stock from the sales. However, the risk is if you don't make the sales you expect, you still have to pay the bill.

While it is nice to have the flexibility that terms provide, it is also a good way to increase debt quickly. In the years since the economy slowed, getting terms has become much more difficult.

2. Building Your Own Computers

If you are interested in selling prebuilt computers for your customers, the best way to go about this is to build them yourself. Since you will need to warranty the computers you build (we offer a one-year warranty with an option for the customer to purchase an extended warranty for up to three years), you'll want to know they're built right. To that end, ensure that you have high-quality parts that are less likely to fail.

To price these machines, build in a 20 to 30 percent margin on any new computer sales. If you offer computers for less than this, you may have problems when you try to complete warranty repairs.

However, if you are a small shop, do not build multiple computers at once. Generally, keep a two-week stock on hand. Remember, you can upgrade the machine as needed or downgrade it if necessary.

3. Auctions

Auctions can be a place to find low-priced computers or they can be a place to get taken advantage of. In general, if you are newly entering the computer field, stay away from auctions. If you have extensive diagnostic experience, you may be able to purchase items at an auction. Just be aware that the best systems are not usually sold at auctions. Many computers are sold this way because the original owners know the machines are missing hard drives, have bad motherboards, and no usable RAM.

4. What to Do If You Are Taken Advantage of by a Vendor

There are many different ways that you can try to get your money returned or a problem resolved. However, it is always easier to prevent a problem than to try to resolve it later. Here are some ways to try and recover your money:

- **Escalate the issue:** The best way to begin is to call the company and try to work out a resolution. Depending on the problem, you may be able to be compensated even if you can't get your money back. Some vendors have return programs, others will issue a refund, and still others will give you credit toward your next purchase. Most companies will try to work with you and if they can't, asking to speak to a manager or supervisor may get you the desired results.

- **Stop the payment:** Depending on the type of problem you have, you may be able to stop payment to the vendor. For instance, if a vendor has taken payment and has not provided the product or service, this is a great way to handle the problem. This is the easiest to do when you have paid by credit card. You can simply call your card company and let them know what has happened. They will be able to reverse the charges and give you your money back. If you paid by check, your bank can stop the payment as long as the check hasn't cleared. Of course, if you paid by cash or wire transfer, you will not be able to stop the payment.

- **Better Business Bureau complaints:** Lodge a complaint with the Better Business Bureau (BBB). If the vendor will not handle your complaint to your satisfaction, you have the opportunity to lodge a complaint with the BBB. While this will work to escalate your issue with some companies, if the company already has a poor BBB rating, it will probably not respond.

- **Small claims court:** If you have a complaint against a business in your area, it may be possible to take it to small claims court. Of course, this gets more complicated for businesses outside of your area or when purchases were made over the Internet.

- **Civil lawsuit:** When a company defaults on a contract, it may be possible to contact a lawyer and make a more formal complaint. Of course, the cost associated with the lawyer's fees and the difficulty getting the money back may make this option financially prohibitive.

When will you get your money back? The truth is, you probably won't. Sure, there are many ways to request your money be returned, but getting your money back may prove to be a very difficult situation. If the company refuses to work with you from the beginning, odds are good it doesn't intend to resolve the situation. As a result, you may find that it can take more time, money, and effort to get your money back than you really want to spend.

You may want to "get even" but as a business owner, this may not be in your best interest. Problems like these can easily escalate and be more costly than they are effective. That said, it may be possible to get some publicity around your issue to prevent it from happening to others in the future. For instance, although it isn't likely to resolve your problem, it may be valuable to let others know about your problem. News agencies, local papers, and the like may be interested in companies that are systematically providing poor service. While it won't get you your money back, it will give you the opportunity to prevent it from happening to others and may give you a bit of satisfaction.

11

On-Site
Service
Calls

Very often, customers will call, asking to arrange an on-site visit. The conversation usually begins like this:

Customer: "My computer is not working properly, can I have someone come and fix it?"

Technician: "Sure, when are you available?"

If the technician fails to get any further information before arranging the on-site visit, he or she is doing a disservice to the customer and himself or herself. For instance, is it a problem the technician can fix? We don't know. The problem could be that the Internet is down or could be another mundane problem. While most technicians will charge a customer just to travel to his or her home to give him or her this information, the customer will resent it. We meet people every day that complain about their previous technicians because they were charged for a service call like this.

When a customer calls, take the time to ask a few questions. Find out what the problem is and let the person know what you think caused the issue and what you think will fix the problem. While you don't want to commit to anything (let the customer know this is just a guesstimate), you do want to show that you understand the problem.

1. Discuss Payment Terms

Before you agree to go on-site, let the customer know the on-site service price and the minimum service charge. Also, ask how he or she will be paying. Believe it or not, there are customers who request on-site services and don't ever intend to pay.

For example, one customer called us about a computer she purchased from us a few months earlier and requested we come to look at it. When we asked the question, "How will you be paying for this today?" She replied, "Paying? Why should I pay for this, the computer is under warranty?" We then had to explain that the warranty policy did not extend to free on-site service and, if she wanted a warranty repair, she would have to bring the computer to the store. She immediately cancelled the on-site.

2. Whether or Not You Should Go On-site

Once you know what the problem is, you may realize that the problem will take too long to handle on-site. For instance, reloading a Vista operating system (OS) can take hours. Installing the OS, completing all the updates, and finding all the necessary drivers is a long process. However, a simple driver update can be done remotely without you ever being on-site. So, how do you know what to do?

In general, if you won't be spending the majority of your time "working" on the computer (you will be waiting for scans to run or something similar), we recommend completing the work at your location and charging a flat fee. If you spend all your time focused on one computer, an on-site or remote repair is appropriate.

Our technicians usually tell our business customers when we think they would benefit from an in-store flat service versus an on-site hourly service. If the in-store service is less expensive, we also offer the option of us coming to pick up the computer and dropping it off again (at our usual hourly rate), or allowing the customer's employee to drop it off instead. In general, most companies prefer to drop it off themselves than to incur our pickup and delivery charge.

In Table 3, we show where we recommend doing each type of work. Of course, Table 3 is just a guide. As you learn more about your individual customers and get more experience with the types of calls you will receive you will be able to tune your business model to meet your customers' needs.

 As a business owner, you can turn down a customer at any time. If you have reason to believe a customer won't pay, has threatened you or another employee in the past, or seems overly hostile, simply turn down the on-site. Never go into a situation if you aren't comfortable with the customer.

3. Tools to Bring to Every On-Site

In general, you should have a toolbox for your on-sites. This will allow you to make sure that you bring what you need to every job. If you try to pull tools that you use every day in your repairs from your on-site toolbox, odds are good that something will be missing when you go to leave for a job. Therefore, make an on-site toolbox and make sure that the tools remain with the box.

Checklist 4 will help you to organize and prepare an on-site kit.

Before you leave each job, use the toolbox checklist to ensure that you have gathered everything from the on-site visit. Using this checklist may seem silly, but it will save you money compared to purchasing additional "lost" equipment or paying for gas to return to a customer's home to pick up the forgotten part. We lost a very expensive DeWALT powered screwdriver because one of our techs forgot it at a job.

TABLE 3
WHERE TO COMPLETE WORK

Type of Problem	Where to Work	Reasoning
Viruses	Your location	In general, removing viruses is tedious and annoying. Since so much of your time will be spent waiting for the computer to be scanned, this service can take hours if not days. Most of the time, you won't be "working" on the computer to justify an hourly charge.
Network connectivity	On-site	This is a great example of something you need to be on-site to resolve. Network issues can be traced to other computers, servers, and routers, so connectivity is nearly impossible to fix without being there.
Computer doesn't turn on	Your location	If a computer doesn't turn on at all, you know there are hardware problems. While it may be as easy as replacing a power supply, this issue could easily turn into replacing the hard drive with a full wipe and reload. If that is the case, it will be easier to do this at your location.
Printing problem	Remote access	When users can't print, you may want to start by doing a remote call. In some cases, the user has simply failed to install his or her drivers. In other cases, they are not seeing the printer at all. This is an example of a time that you can start with a remote call but may need to follow up with an on-site visit.

3.1 Up selling with additional items

Once you are at an on-site, you may find that the computer is not running as well as it could. Maybe the hard drive is almost full or maybe it doesn't have enough RAM to run the user's applications. Whatever it is, some of these problems can be solved quickly if you have the products on hand for the sale. Some items you may want to take with you to up sell to the customers include:

- **Antivirus:** As you start working with customers you will find that many people don't have or don't use antivirus. If you are there to do work, you should always check the customer's antivirus status and offer him or her antivirus with installation for some fixed cost.

- **RAM:** Customers constantly complain about slow computers. One of the easiest ways to fix this problem is with additional RAM if you have it. Make sure to

CHECKLIST 4
ON-SITE TOOLBOX

- ☐ On-site forms (including clipboard, pens, and any other forms you may need to get the appropriate approvals and payments)
- ☐ Power supply tester
- ☐ Standard 400-watt PSU
- ☐ Extra power supply
- ☐ Software disks — you will need some CDs to complete repairs. The following software disks should be part of your toolkit:
  - ○ Hiren's BootCD
  - ○ A system boot disk
- ☐ Small screwdriver set (for laptops)
- ☐ Power screwdriver (get one with a torque on it)
- ☐ *Your* flash drive (have all your system images on one flash drive)
- ☐ External CD drive
- ☐ Blank DVDs (just in case you want to do a data transfer)
- ☐ Extra power cord
- ☐ Extra CAT 5 network cable
- ☐ Other: _____
- ☐ Other: _____

bring multiple types (e.g., DDR, DDR2, DDR3) in multiple sizes. It may seem like a significant investment, but it will cost you less than $500 for your "full stock" and will allow you to make additional sales with little additional work.

- **Hard drives:** While you probably don't want to reimage a hard drive at a client's site, if he or she is running out of space, it is easy to offer to add an additional drive to the desktop. In general, you only need two or three hard drives

and only desktop models. Once again, this is covered with an investment of as little as $200 and is a simple installation that can earn extra dollars.

- **Flash drives:** Bring one or two flash drives with you to sell. Sometimes they are necessary.

- **External hard drive cases:** Occasionally, a customer has an old computer which he or she no longer wants, but the person does want the data. Keeping an external hard drive case on hand lets you give the customer his or her data without having the work and risk of a data transfer. Plus, you can offer to recycle the rest of the old machine for him or her (which can bring you additional dollars).

- **Surge protector and voltage regulator:** If you run into a power supply that is blown (which you will), chances are the customer doesn't have a surge protector on the system and he or she certainly doesn't have a voltage regulator. Either way, to prevent a recurrence, the customer should get one or the other.

Make sure that all of your items available for resale are properly packaged and labeled. Your customer will be more comfortable buying these products from you if he or she realizes they are new and still in the box. Also, do not feel like you have to take all the products into the customer's site. It is perfectly acceptable to leave them in your car and just bring in a price list to aid in your discussions.

4. Special Order Items

Of course, there are other items, such as computers, laptops, and servers that you can have your customers order. While many customers may want to buy a computer, in general, it is better to leave these at your business location. If they want a computer, you can offer complete delivery and installation for an additional charge (we usually charge one hour of labor for this service).

Also, if the customers are ordering custom equipment that you don't normally keep in stock (even if it is just a new computer), make sure to get some part of the payment in advance. If you think it would be easy to resell, you can take a deposit of just 50 percent. However, if it is a custom part that is very specialized (e.g., laptop battery or slimline power supply), the customer should prepay the full amount. Too often, people order items and change their minds. In the case of custom parts, this can be expensive for a small business.

12
Warranties

If you are selling computers, your customers will expect you to offer a warranty on the system. Therefore, you will need to think about what type of policy your business wants to have. Some companies cover shipping on warranty work — sending the customer a prepaid shipping label, whereas others ask the customer to pay for shipping. Some warranties are full no-fault warranties while others only cover repairs for malfunctioning parts. You need to decide what your business will or will not cover.

We choose to cover only those parts that are found to be defective, not parts that are broken due to abuse, negligence, or customer error. For example, if a customer comes in with a bad motherboard that has leaking caps, it is usually covered under the warranty. However, when a customer comes in with loose VGA connectors on the motherboard, and he or she has admitted the cables are constantly kicked, that is not covered by our warranty.

The problem is that most customers believe that almost everything should be covered by a warranty, including damage they cause. Therefore, in order to make sure you avoid customer conflicts, document your warranty in advance. List everything you cover and don't cover and, if you want to, include explanations. If you aren't sure what should be in a warranty in your area, have your lawyer review the document as well. Sample 9 is a type of document used at our stores.

1. Warranty Seals

Warranty seals are somewhat controversial but also very helpful. A warranty seal is a sticker that goes across the computer in such a way to ensure that if the computer was opened and tampered with you can tell. They are great reminders to customers that computers have fragile parts, and that tampering with the system when you aren't an experienced technician could result in damaging it.

A typical warranty seal is made on special stickers that are difficult to remove and look something like Sample 10.

The controversy arises when a knowledgeable person wants to make a simple and standard upgrade. Has the person really broken the warranty by removing that seal and upgrading the memory?

SAMPLE 9
COMPUTER LIMITED WARRANTY

YOUR COMPUTER OUTLET STORES
COMPUTER LIMITED WARRANTY

FREE TUNE-UP — $49 VALUE!

This limited warranty includes a *free* computer tune-up every 6 months for the length of the limited warranty.

Warranty Period

Warranty is valid from the date of purchase from Your Computer Outlet Stores. One of the following warranties is provided:

- FREE 1-year warranty — with new computer purchase
- FREE 30-day warranty — with off-lease computer purchase

The following extended warranties are available and must be purchased on the same date and receipt as the computer under warranty — Please initial one option:

___ **Extended 6-month warranty — $25 (adds 6 months)**
___ **Extended 1-year warranty — $50 (adds 1 year)**
___ **Extended 2-year warranty — $100 (adds 2 years)**
___ **Extended 3-year warranty — $150 (adds 3 years)**
___ **NO additional warranty selected**

The warranty for repaired or replaced parts is the remainder of the warranty period or 30 days, whichever is longer. All implied warranties are limited to the duration of this limited warranty.

What Is Covered

This limited warranty covers defects in parts and workmanship on computers sold by Your Computer Outlet Stores.

What We Will Do

We will provide you with a free diagnostic review to determine if the computer repair is covered by this limited warranty. We will repair, or if repair is not possible, we will replace any defective parts at no charge for materials or labor, except as excluded below.

What Is Not Covered

This warranty is not an unconditional guarantee. The following parts and types of damages are not covered by this limited warranty:

- Specialty glass casing, lighting, and fans.
- Normal wear and tear on component parts, moving parts, and wheels. These parts will typically show wear with use over time, and eventually may need to be refurbished or replaced.
- Any computer on which the serial number has been defaced modified, or removed.
- Any computer on which the tamper-proof stickers have been removed.
- Damage, deterioration, or malfunction resulting from —
  - accident, abuse, mishandling, misuse, neglect, fire, water, lightning, or other acts of nature;
  - unauthorized product modification or failure to follow instructions included with the computer;
  - repair or attempted repair by anyone not authorized by Your Computer Outlet Stores;
  - shipment of the computer to us for evaluation and repair (these claims must be made to the shipping carrier); and
  - Any other causes that do not relate to a product defect including build-up damage from smoking around your computer system.
- All peripheral equipment (e.g., printers, scanners, speakers, monitors) to your computer. See the separate manufacturer's warranties for the equipment.
- Any damage to your computer, including the motherboard, power supply, hard drive, etc, due to faulty wiring or power fluctuations within your home (e.g., a blown power supply and motherboard indicate a power fluctuation not a manufacturer defect). **We recommend that all computers be protected by an Uninterruptible Power Supply (UPS) with Automatic Voltage Regulation (AVR).** A surge protector will not protect you from dips in your electricity and will not provide voltage regulation. High and low dips in voltage can cause severe damage to your hard drive and power supply even though a surge protector is in place.
- Any software or any damages caused by software. Consumers should always check that the software you are about to install is compatible with the specifications of your computer. All computers are tested and in proper working order when they leave Your Computer Outlet Stores. The only way software can be corrupted is as a direct result of the user (e.g., if you install a program such as AOL and your computer does not run correctly after installation of said software, that is a direct result of software incompatibility and/or user error).

We will always be happy to provide you with prompt high-quality repair service for the above types of damages; however, hourly labor charges will apply and there will be charges for any necessary replacement parts.

Warranty Requirements

- The warranty is nontransferable — it is enforceable only by the original consumer purchaser.
- The computer must be accompanied by a proof of purchase in the form of the original receipt and this warranty.
- We seal all computers we sell with tamper-proof stickers on each side. These stickers are to ensure that you do not open the case and cause damage to the internal parts of your system. If for any reason the tamper-proof warranty seals are broken, your warranty is null and void immediately. NO EXCEPTIONS.

Exclusion of Damages

Our sole obligation and liability under this warranty is limited to the repair or replacement of a defective product at our option. We are not liable to you or any third party for any incidental or consequential damage, including, but not limited to, damages resulting from interruption of service and loss of business, or liability in turn relating to this product or resulting from its use or possession.

How to Obtain Warranty Service

You must bring your computer with intact tamper proof warranty seals and a copy of the proof of purchase (this warranty and the original receipt) to the Your Computer Outlet Stores location of original purchase. During the warranty period any defective parts will be repaired or, if repair is not possible, will be replaced at no charge for parts or labor. All warranty work must be performed at Your Computer Outlet Stores. There are no house calls, pickups, or deliveries. NO EXCEPTIONS. We are able to provide you with competitive prices and timely service because our technicians work strictly on an in-store basis. If you have moved out of a Your Computer Outlet Stores local area then you must ship your computer for evaluation or repair. We will not be responsible for any shipping charges you incur or any damages from shipping. If you are shipping, be sure to include a copy of your original receipt as proof of purchase. You must arrange for payment of the return shipping charges before any repairs are completed.

Out-of-Warranty Service

If a repair is required after this warranty period or there are damages to your computer that are not included in this limited warranty, there will be a charge for service and parts. Bring your computer to Your Computer Outlet Stores for a free diagnostic service and estimate on needed repairs.

Your Rights under State Law

This warranty gives you specific legal rights, and you may also have other rights which vary from state to state.

**Your Computer Outlet Stores thanks you
for your patronage.**

SAMPLE 10
WARRANTY SEAL

WARNING

OPENING THIS MACHINE MAY DAMAGE YOUR COMPUTER AND VOID YOUR WARRANTY.

In the past, vendors have said that they won't repair computers that have this seal damaged or mutilated in any way. However, over the years, there has been some discussion about the legality of this policy. For instance, customers often upgrade a computer's graphics card, memory, or hard drive. Should these standard upgrades really be considered violation of warranty? The answer is no. In general, making a standard upgrade to a computer is not considered to be a warranty violation even if it did damage the warranty seal. Yet, companies continue to use these seals. Why? Well, to be honest, it is because most people will damage their computer if they start "messing around" when they notice a problem. Therefore, these seals are important warning labels for most customers.

At our company, while we do have warranty seals, we also honor our warranty if the seal is broken but there has been no abuse. We have kept the seals to remind the average customer that playing around with the machine could break it and could void the warranty. Also, we place our name and phone number on the seal to remind the customer that the repair may be under warranty.

2. Keeping Warranty Costs Reduced

While a warranty will cost your business some money each time a repair needs to be completed and a part needs to be replaced, there are many ways to offset these costs. In some cases, you may find that a customer comes in for warranty work and that work will bring in additional sales!

2.1 Make sure that the computer is under warranty

Just because a computer was purchased from your company and it has a problem, doesn't mean it is under warranty. However, that doesn't mean customers won't try to insist it is under warranty. Before you start exploring the customer's problem, get the warranty information if he or she says it is a warranty repair. The customer should be able to provide both the receipt and the warranty information. While you can keep this type of information on record for the customer, remember, this is the customer's responsibility, *not* yours. If the warranty has expired, make sure the customer understands that you can diagnose the computer, but the repair will not be covered under the expired warranty.

2.2 Software problems are almost *never* under warranty

One honest customer misconception is that software problems are under warranty. I had a customer insist that viruses should be covered since that's why she bought a new computer, so that she wouldn't get these annoying viruses! To my knowledge there is no hardware manufacturer anywhere that would warranty a machine against getting viruses. If a computer comes in "running slowly" and turns out to have viruses, the virus removal is not covered under warranty. Therefore, you can offer the customer the service, but before you begin, make sure he or she understands that this type of work is *not* covered by the warranty and there will be a charge for the service.

There are a few cases in which software could be covered. For instance, if you forgot to install the drivers on a new computer, this would be covered by most warranties (and good service policies). Other than that, almost everything else is not included.

2.3 Abuse should *not* be covered

One of the most damaging things a customer can do to his or her computer is smoke in the same room. We have seen so many computers that are full of dust and debris because the owners smoked in the same room, or left them in very dusty, hot rooms. In other cases, customers have hooked the machine directly into the wall outlet without a voltage regulator or surge protector.

In cases like these, the computer has been abused and there is no manufacturing defect. Therefore, this type of damage is typically not covered by a warranty. Make sure to show the customer the overwhelming smoke dust or the damage to multiple parts to prove your assertion. Otherwise, it could appear as if you don't stand behind your product.

2.4 Parts can be replaced at little or no cost to you

Once you have determined that the computer is under warranty and that the problem is also under warranty, you should try to complete the repair at the lowest cost possible. This usually begins by choosing reliable vendors and well-made products to sell to your customer. Whether you choose to buy or build your computers, make sure you find quality products that come with warranties of their own.

For instance, our computers are custom built with parts we know are reliable and are created by companies that stand by their products. As a result, when a part breaks, we can return it directly to the vendor. This is typically done with a Return Merchandise Authorization (RMA). The result is that the vendor replaces the part and all we have to pay is the cost of shipping to the vendor. Since we usually do this once a month, the costs are often only a few dollars for a replacement motherboard or hard drive!

Make sure to complete RMAs at least once a month. Many manufacturers change their products a few times a year to make sure that products that are too old and are broken because of normal wear and tear are not able to be returned as new parts.

If your vendor won't take back the part, check with the manufacturer. Oftentimes, the parts you used to build the computer will come with warranties. Many large companies will accept these parts and replace them with a new part of same or better value. For instance, if you look at the Seagate website, you can enter the serial number of a hard drive and discover if it is under warranty. If it is, you can return that product to Seagate without even finding the receipt!

With some good record keeping and by purchasing high-quality parts, you can keep the costs for replacement parts to almost nothing.

3. Look for Up Selling Opportunities

The customer may be in the store for a replacement part, but that doesn't mean that there aren't other opportunities for up selling. For instance, we allow our customers to purchase a three-year warranty. When a customer comes in with a three-year-old computer under warranty, there may be additional up selling opportunities. Does the customer want more RAM? If we are replacing the hard drive anyway, does he or she want to spend a few extra dollars to get a larger drive? How about the latest and greatest operating system since we have to wipe and reload anyway? Sometimes

when your customers are already getting some of the work for free they may be willing to spend a few extra dollars for the better part.

4. Don't Let the Warranty Scope Creep

So, the hard drive failed on your customer's new computer. What are you obligated to repair? According to your warranty, all you owe the customer is a new hard drive. However, the customer is furious. All of her applications, photos, and documents were on that machine! She wants a full data recovery. What are you going to do?

In general, making sure you have a clearly outlined warranty policy is the first step in clearing up this kind of a problem. However, in general, this is your decision. You could, if you want to help the customer, try to recover what you can. However, be careful of scope creep. Once these things start, they tend to grow. For example, if you recover her data, are you also going to try to get her application keys? If you are, will you reinstall all the free apps she had installed as well? What about her antivirus? The issue is that once you allow a little bit of scope creep it's hard to figure out where to stop, so keep your warranty work limited to the scope of your warranty.

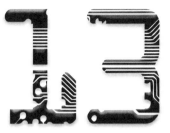

1.3

Provide Great Customer Service

If your customers like you, they will tell all of their friends. Unfortunately, if they don't like you, they will still tell all of their friends.

How do you keep your business growing instead of shrinking? One of the best ways to grow your business is through fantastic customer service. Having a positive attitude, a fast turnaround time, and high-quality work will convince your customers that you are a great company with which to do business. Our stores in Arizona don't do any advertising. We don't pay for any ads, coupons, or product placement. The reason is that once we built our business, it continued to grow through customer referrals. Most of our new customers come as recommendations from other customers. This means that we continue to get new business and grow without any financial investment! Great customer service is like that.

With a repair business, your customer service starts as soon as you get the call and will continue until the problem is resolved. Since you want your customers to call you with all their computer problems and questions, you want to build a strong relationship throughout the entire problem process. Remember, customers are usually frustrated and annoyed when they have computer problems, so it is always your job to make sure that they have a positive experience.

 Customer service in the computer business begins before you ever see the customer or touch the person's computer.

1. Tips to Provide *Great* Customer Service

One of the most amazing things we have observed over the years is that a technician's attitude can either grow or sink the business. We have hired people who were great with customers, and people come in asking for them by name. Other technicians have been so bad that after they left, customers returned saying that they were glad they were finally gone. To keep your business thriving, make sure to follow the simple rules outlined in the next few sections.

1.1 Plain language works best

Use plain language so that you are understood by your customer. If the computer is having a problem connecting to the WAN, don't use technical jargon by referring to the IEEE 802.11 standard when you could simply tell the customer his or her WiFi isn't working.

In general, using technical jargon is a mistake many new technicians make. While they may believe this makes them look knowledgeable and experienced, it usually doesn't. Most customers simply see the technician as condescending and obnoxious.

1.2 Answer the phone politely

Make sure to answer the phone with a smile and be upbeat and positive. Remember that when you get a call, the customer has a problem and he or she wants to know that the person he or she is talking to can fix the problem, and is not someone who will make it worse. A positive attitude is a great way to convince a customer he or she is in good hands.

1.3 Empathize with your customer

When a customer brings you an issue, be sympathetic and understanding. Should he or she have known to back up the hard drive? Sure, but that doesn't mean that you should tell the customer this when he or she realizes he or she just lost all the family photos from the last ten years. Furthermore, even though you may be happy to have found the issue, a bad hard drive is not good news for anyone. When you relate the problem, make sure you don't appear too "happy" to have found the problem. This could be misunderstood as a lack of empathy.

1.4 Providing solutions, not just problems

Let's face it; everyone who brings a computer to a computer repair shop has a problem. They aren't paying you to tell them what's wrong. They already know that they have an issue; they are paying you for a solution.

When you call a customer to let him or her know you found the cause of his or her stress, don't dwell on the issue. Immediately, provide what you believe the solution should be. For instance, when you call about a bad hard drive, you should mention that you can try a data recovery. If the customer has viruses, immediately start discussing how you can complete a virus removal. You can tell you are doing this well when you are driving the conversation forward. If the customer has to ask, "Well, what can you do to fix it?" You need to practice the skill of providing solutions and not just problems.

1.5 Keeping the customer in the loop

When you are working with customers, you need to be honest about what is happening with their computer. Unfortunately, most people have assumptions about computer repair. They think that as soon as they bring their computer in to a technician it will be serviced immediately. They sometimes believe repairs are easy and will be done faster than is really possible. The best way to manage these unrealistic expectations is to communicate often and honestly with your customers.

As soon as they walk in, let them know how long a diagnostic usually takes. Once you have identified the problem and the probable solution, make sure to give them a realistic (not optimistic) estimate of how long it will take to fix. If you run into any issues that are going to extend the time it takes to fix the issue, call them and let them know immediately. The more interaction you have with the customers, the more understanding they will be.

2. When Something Goes Wrong

No matter how hard you try to make sure everything goes smoothly, there are always problems that will arise. Working parts will break, vendors will be late, and work will take longer than you expected. However, how you handle these problems will make the difference between having a very happy customer and a very hostile customer.

I cannot count the number of times a customer came into the store with a computer and we have identified the failed part as a motherboard or another part. Unfortunately, what kills one component in a computer often kills others. Just because the CPU seems to be working, doesn't mean that it is. One of the hardest conversations you can have is when you have to call the customer and let him or her know that *another* part of the computer is broken. This conversation will be easier if you followed the steps for doing a complete diagnostic. Unfortunately, what you did *before* this call matters almost as much as the call itself. For instance:

- The customer should have known that there were risks that other parts of the computer could be broken, so this customer shouldn't be blindsided when you call.

- You should be working on the computer in a timely manner. This means that you didn't wait days or weeks to test the computer and find additional problems. If you call within the first day or so, customers are more likely to believe the problem is part of the original issue and not something you did.

Assuming that these things have been done, when you call, let the customer know what additional tests you ran and what you found. Then, as soon as you tell the customer about the broken part, make sure to also tell him or her what can be done to repair the computer. This lets the customer know that there are still options. Give him or her a few minutes to decide but make sure to have the person agree or disagree with you doing additional repairs. Once another problem is found, it may no longer be worthwhile to fix the machine or perhaps the price will increase. Make sure the customer has a clear picture of what the new cost will be, and get a clear confirmation of whether or not he or she wants to make the recommended repairs.

3. Handling Returns

In general, there aren't too many returns in the computer repair field. Service is obviously not returnable (how could you take back a virus removal?) and most issues with parts are handled through the manufacturer, not the store directly. As a result, there is limited customer conflict around returns. The most commonly returned items are the computers themselves. Therefore, it is important to have a solid policy in place about computer returns.

Since computers are delicate electronics, it is possible for customers to damage the equipment and then return it. Therefore, if you allow returns, you don't want to let a return be available for too long. At our store, we only allow new computers to be returned within seven days and there is a 15 percent restocking fee. The restocking fee allows us to cover the costs of the credit card transaction fees, testing the computer before resale, and wiping and reloading the operating system. To be clear, this policy is posted in our store *and* written on the receipts. However, this still doesn't stop problems from occurring.

The worst return problem we ran into was a customer who called saying that she wanted to return her computer because "it doesn't send email attachments." Since we often help our customers with problems like this for free, we offered to help her with her email program and show her how to add the attachment herself. She agreed and we taught her how to send attachments. The next day, she called back insisting that she needed to return the computer. When we asked her what the problem was, she became irritated and started yelling that she just wanted to return it. We asked when she purchased the machine — it was more than two months earlier. We then explained that according to our company's return policy we could not accept the computer back after two months. Our return policy clearly stated that it had to be returned in the first seven days. At that point, she just started yelling that we had to take the computer and she expected us to go to her home and pick it up! Needless to say, we ended our relationship with this unreasonable customer. Unfortunately, no matter what you do, there will always be customers like this. However, making your policies clear in writing makes it much easier to handle these problems when they do arise.

4. Customer Lessons You Need to Learn

There are many lessons we have learned over the years, which are discussed in the following sections.

4.1 People lie!

Just because a customer reports something is working, doesn't mean that it really is. Sometimes, he or she really doesn't know what is broken and, other times, he or she is trying to hide a problem hoping that you will repair it because you will think you broke it!

One customer came in for a free 15-minute diagnostic. Her issue was that the system was running slowly. We worked with her for a few minutes and realized that she only had 256K of RAM. We offered her RAM and to install it for an additional fee. She chose to purchase the RAM and install it herself. The next day she returned with the computer saying she changed her mind and that she wanted us to do the RAM installation instead. Although she had just been in, we started the entire diagnostic again, beginning with turning on the computer. When we tried to turn it on, nothing happened. We checked the power supply and it was no longer working. It was then that she mentioned that she tried to install the RAM and had run into a problem. So, she removed the RAM and brought the machine back to us. If we hadn't started that technical review all over again, she could have claimed that we broke the power supply.

Completing a full-tech inspection *before* you start working on the computer doesn't just save the customer; it can save your business as well.

4.2 Customers don't always know what they need

There are times customers walk in the door with their computer as well as their diagnosis. They may say, "My computer has viruses and I want a virus removal." Or, "My operating system is corrupt; can you do a Windows repair?"

Just because they are using repair terms doesn't mean they have done a professional diagnosis.

Before you believe any of these customers, make sure to complete your own testing. Check-in the computer and begin your entire test process. You can start checking for what they believe isn't working, but make sure that it doesn't influence your review. We have had customers that come in complaining about viruses because they can't get on the Internet. After a brief inspection, we have found their wireless card was turned off on their laptop. Another customer was sure he needed an OS repair, but his computer had a failing hard drive.

To a layperson, the symptoms may all look the same, but the customer is counting on you to get it right. After all, if you do the work the customer requests and it doesn't fix the problem, he or she will certainly blame you instead of himself or herself.

4.3 Almost all customers care about their data

One of the hardest things to learn is to speak like a layperson when you are talking with a customer. Oftentimes, the customer's data will be put at risk, or sometimes with a wipe and reload, the data is deleted completely. Most of your customers will want to keep the data from their computer. If the customer agrees to lose his or her data too quickly, chances are he or she hasn't understood what you are asking. For example:

Technician: "Is it okay if we wipe your hard drive?"

Customer (without pausing): "Yeah, sure, whatever it takes to get the computer running right."

Even if the customer has signed all the right forms and given you verbal approval, odds are good he or she has not understood the meaning of what you just asked. When it comes to data deletion, make sure you are *very* clear about what is happening and why. A better way to ask the question would be:

Technician: "If we do this, it will *delete everything* on your computer. This means that you will lose all your photos, documents, and any Internet bookmarks or passwords saved on this computer as well as all your programs such as Microsoft Office, accounting software such as TurboTax, or any other games or data on your computer."

At that point, if the customer agrees, you know that he or she understands exactly what will be happening and what will be lost if the work is completed. If the customer doesn't want to lose his or her data or programs, you can discuss other options and alternatives. Even then, make sure the customer signs a form stating he or she understands *everything* will be gone.

4.4 Do-it-yourselfers can be costly

When you start getting regular customers, you may find that some of these people may be do-it-yourselfers. They may have started working on their computer and then ran into a problem that was too difficult for them to resolve. Many times people will ask to have these computers diagnosed, but these individuals can be expensive for your business. For instance, some of these people will want to talk about their computer indefinitely. They want to know what they did wrong, how to do it right, and more. While these conversations can be interesting at first, they will take your time and often, not give you any return. If you are at an on-site, they may think that you shouldn't charge for the time you spent "talking shop" and will only want you to bill for your repair time. At your office, they may hang around, wanting to learn what they can and then make the repairs themselves.

The problem with these people is that they will distract you from work and the more you tell them, the more they expect you will help them. Since they aren't technicians, this means that they start expecting that you will talk them through their problems for free.

One of our technicians came up with a great way of discouraging this type of behavior. When a customer brings in a computer that needs to be repaired, if he or she asks, "Can I do that myself"? We now ask, "Are you comfortable making modifications to your BIOS?" If the person is, then it is likely he or she can handle any problem he or she may encounter. If he or she is not, he or she will realize that while most of the work sounds simple, sometimes the problem is deeper than it seems.

4.5 People are willing to pay *before* the problem is fixed

Always discuss price *before* you do work. If you wait until after the computer is fixed to mention the price, you will run into situations in which you have completed the work and the customer either doesn't have the money, doesn't want the service, or simply thinks he or she can reduce the price.

For example, a customer brings in a computer that is running slowly and during the diagnosis (which at our store is free), we determine the machine just needs more RAM. While the computer is still open, we tell the customer that we can double the RAM for $80. We explain that

the costs are $15 for the installation, $59 for the part, and $6 for the tax. Usually, the customer agrees, and we complete the part installation in front of the person and allow him or her to test the machine before he or she leaves. If the customer is happy with the speed, he or she pays the $80. If not, we can remove the RAM and there is no charge. (I have never had to remove the RAM.)

Let's say that you complete the upgrade first and then ask the customer if he or she wants to "keep it like that" for $80. Now you have already completed the "service" portion without his or her approval, so the likely question is, "Why do I need to pay the $15-service fee when it only took you a minute?" Or, since the customer just watched you do the install, he or she may ask, "Couldn't I have done that myself?" (Never mind that the person didn't know the difference between the RAM stick and the hard drive before he or she walked in.) Either way, you have wasted your time and now have a customer issue. Getting approval for the work in advance prevents problems like these.

4.6 People will want custom work done for free

When we first started the business, we were eager to get any new customer we could. As a result, we often made concessions for customers that wanted things "just a little different" or didn't quite have enough money. Inevitably, every time we went around our policies to help these customers, they were still not happy. For instance, one customer complained that the case we sold her for her new computer was too large. (Obviously she had to see the case before she bought it, but hey, why not help her out?) She made a big fuss, so we ordered a new smaller case and transferred all the components for free. This time, instead of complaining about the size, she complained that it still weighed too much. When we refused to move the system a third time, she fought us and complained about the service.

I know this may sound like a gross generalization, but it comes from years and years of experience. While it may sound like an aberration, unfortunately, the situation is all too common. For some reason, people who are very particular and want to customize their orders are also more likely to complain about how much custom work was completed — for *free*.

14

Extra
Sources of
Income

As a business owner, you have the opportunity of adding other sources of income to your business. As you work, keep an eye out for new services and products your customers request. What starts as a small side income could expand in a direction you never expected. This chapter lists some of the side businesses that could mean big revenue for you.

1. Maintenance Plans

If you get regular business customers, you may be able to interest them in a maintenance plan. What this means is that you will arrive at their place of business at a set time each month (or sometimes week) to handle any on-site issues they may have. For small, growing businesses, this may be an inexpensive option as opposed to having your own on-site staff. For you, this source of income can provide regular revenue.

2. Computer Recycling

In most areas, you are not allowed to throw away technology equipment. In some places, homeowners have to bring their old technology equipment to special disposal areas. These types of laws make it difficult for most people to get rid of old, worn-out computers. However, when computers are being repaired or inspected, you will often find customers with computers they no longer want and don't want to bother disposing of themselves.

You can offer your customers a chance to recycle their computers with you. If they no longer want the equipment, taking it off their hands is great for you and for them. There are many things that you can do to recycle the equipment, as described in the following sections.

2.1 Repair and sell

Although it may not be cost effective for the customer to repair an older machine, for you, it may be just fine. If the person needs to wipe and reload a computer, it will often cost him or her between $100 and $200 even if the computer is still an old machine. However, as a technician, completing a wipe and reload may be simple and you can turn around and sell the computer.

Completing repairs gives you a usable computer that you can sell as a used machine. Just make sure to fully test the computer before you do any software repairs. If any parts fail, it may be worth keeping parts of the computer instead of repairing it.

2.2 Keep the computer for parts

The computer may be in bad shape, but there are often parts that you can reuse. Does it have RAM? Is the power supply in working order? Does it have a good CPU? Keeping some used computers on hand means that you have an inventory of used parts for repairs. Sure, they aren't able to be sold for as much as a new system, but considering they cost you nothing, sales of any of these parts are pure profit. In general, stripping a computer for parts can be very profitable and even a nonworking computer can make you $50 to $100 after the parts have been fully tested and resold.

RAM is generally good in the system. Very rarely is bad RAM the source of computer failures. With that said, you should still run tests (e.g., QTP) on each stick individually before making it available for resale. Because used RAM is as durable as new, you can often sell used RAM for just $10 less than the price of new. In Q1 of 2011, a stick of 1G DDR2 used could be sold for as much as $35 and would save the customer between $10 and $15 off of the price of new!

Power supplies are one of the most common parts of a computer that have problems. This part needs to be tested thoroughly before resale. Further, a normal power supply tester may not be enough, since most of these testers don't test all the connectors. If you place a nonworking power supply in an otherwise good system, you can short out working parts. While I wouldn't be opposed to using used power supplies to build used systems, selling them to customers without having fully tested them is a risk.

Hard drives are another easy part to test and resell. Once again, QTP has a testing tool which allows you to check every part of the drive as well as the drive speed. If the drive is running too slowly, or if the drive fails, it should not be resold — even if it works. However, if it works, used hard drives can be sold for as much as $20 for a 20G drive, or $55 for an 80G drive! Just remember, before you sell any used hard drive, it should be wiped clean of old data.

2.3 Sell the parts on eBay or Craigslist

In some cases, you will find that customers have given you specialty computers or laptops for recycling. Since these computers vary greatly, it is often worth putting the parts on Craigslist or eBay. Working and tested custom parts are often priced based on availability. For example, an old slimline power supply can run as high as $100 for a used replacement. While this may sound crazy to most of us, their rarity increases the prices.

2.4 Scrap it

Even if every single part of the computer is beyond repair, the computer still has value. Keeping the computer parts and collecting them will allow you to turn them in at scrap prices. Because of the special metals that are used in CPUs and sometimes wiring, you may need to divide the computers into parts. Typically, a pound of CPUs will pay more than a pound of case metal.

Collecting all of the parts together and finding a recycling company in your area will make sure that collecting scrap computers from your customers remains profitable.

3. Website Sales

Since you are going to have a website, you may as well sell your products on the site. Although you may not get much traffic at first, having your products up on a website will serve as one way of tracking your inventory. Plus, if you get news coverage or other publicity, the Web traffic it generates can quickly turn into retail sales!

4. Inventory

To keep things simple, determine what you want to sell. You may just want to limit your online business to a few used or new computers. Or, if you have some free time, you may list every product that you can carry. Unless you are getting a lot of traffic, do not try to keep inventory for these sales. Remember, most people expect Internet orders to take a day or two to ship. That will give you plenty of time to rebuild a machine or find a part if you need to. The cost of keeping a large inventory for Internet sales that never materialize could be expensive.

5. Drop Shipping

Another option is to work with some vendors that are willing to do "drop shipping." What this means is that you put the vendor's products on your website. Your price is the cost the vendor charges you plus the profit you want to make on the vendor's product.

Next, you ensure that shipping and handling is correctly managed. Then, you sell the vendor's products without keeping anything in inventory. When the product is ordered, you simply take the order, and enter it into your vendor's system. Because your vendor does drop shipping it will ship the product directly to the customer from you. This means that instead of showing the vendor's name, it will allow you to provide the receipt for your sale.

For instance, one of my suppliers allows drop shipping with TVs. Let's say that a customer orders a TV on our website for $1,000 including shipping. However, the cost to us, including shipping, is only $900 for our vendor. We then provide the customer's information to the drop shipper and it sends the TV to the customer! Since the warranty for the TV is through the manufacturer and not through the distributer, we shouldn't have to handle any problems with the TV.

The only thing to be aware of is the return policy. Since many vendors don't have an easy return policy, you may need to adopt the same terms. After all, if the customer returns to you a $1,000 TV, you will then have to try to find a way to sell it or swallow your cost of the TV!

6. Website Development and Domain Reseller

Another way to make some extra sales is to offer website development and become a domain reseller. GoDaddy offers a simple program that will allow you to become an official reseller complete with your own website, shopping cart, and the ability to take credit cards. Although this program does have associated yearly fees, it may be worthwhile if you plan to complete enough sales.

Also, if you are going to sell website domains, you may want to offer website design as well. With tools such as WordPress and Joomla! available it's easy to make professional-looking websites that can earn you as much as $500 to $1,000 for most sales.

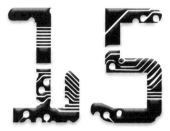

15

Expanding
Your
Business

As more and more customers find out about your business, you may find yourself struggling to keep up with demand. Once this happens, you may find that it is easier to expand than to run yourself ragged with work! There are a few different ways to do this; you could add existing staff, open a retail store of your own, purchase an existing store, or even buy into a franchise. Of course, each of these has different risks and benefits.

1. Hiring Employees

One of the easiest ways to expand your business and maintain control of your brand is to add another employee.

When you are looking for a new team member, there are many different qualities that you will want to find. The most obvious is someone who has the technical skills to complete the job. However, more subtle requirements are often more critical. For instance, if you are hiring a technician, you need to be able to work with him or her. During the interview process you need to determine if you can have a working relationship.

At our stores, we pride ourselves on having down-to-earth technicians that work well with customers. When we interview new techs, my wife found a way to weed out technicians that wouldn't fit with our store. She often asks a new interviewee to help her with some broken-down used system in the back (not a customer computer). Now, the computer problems could range from missing a hard drive to an obscure operating system problem — either way, she acts like she has no idea what is wrong. Watching the way people respond to this test tells us how they will respond to customers. The techs that make it through the test usually diagnose the problem and promptly give her the result. The techs that fail are condescending and rude during the test. One went so far as to ask her how she could be running the store! The point is, the test shows not just skill but also personality.

1.1 Paperwork, paperwork, paperwork

As soon as you hire an employee, you will need to make sure that you have completed all the appropriate employment paperwork. Hiring a new employee means managing all aspects of adding a new employee (e.g., regular payroll, paying payroll taxes, paying workers' compensation, updating insurance). One way to do this with relatively little work is to hire a payroll company. For less than $100 per month, you can get the entire function outsourced and even offer your new employee direct deposit.

There are two documents you should ask your new employees to read and sign:

- **Non-compete agreement:** If the employee leaves your company, this document says that he or she is not allowed to steal your clients and customers.

- **Non-disclosure agreement:** This document ensures that the processes and forms that you use at your business are not allowed to be distributed to your competitors by employees or former employees.

1.2 Training new employees

Once you have chosen who will join your team, the next step is to get the person on board with your system and your processes. Adding an employee is about expanding your business and brand, not finding a new way to do things.

Have your new technician shadow you as you work. This means that instead of him or her working alone, the employee should be watching what you do and how you do it. Teach him or her about your forms, tools, and processes.

1.3 Transitioning your existing clients to new employees

If you have a retail storefront, transitioning your clients to new employees is easy. However, if your business is made up almost entirely of on-site visits, expanding to add new employees

has a risk associated with it. It is possible that a new employee you send to a business client could eventually try to steal your client!

We had a client we did business with regularly. When business started to pick up we found another part-time technician to do the additional on-sites. This seemed to be working well for the first month or two. Then, one of our big clients stopped calling. After a month or so I stopped by just to see how things were going. Guess who was there? Our technician! I severed the relationship with both.

2. Opening a Retail Location

Consider whether you really need to open a retail store. A thriving computer business may not benefit from a retail location. If you are running a successful business out of your home, you may want to consider what changing your business model will entail. Not only will you have additional expenses, but you will also have less flexibility!

In order for the business to make a profit, you need to cover not just your expenses, but also all the overhead fees. Bills for a retail space will include:

- Commercial rent

- Utilities (e.g., water, electricity, gas)

- Cable and internet connectivity

- Security (e.g., roll-down doors, cameras, alarms — computer stores can be targets of break ins)

- Custom signage

- Increased insurance (check with your insurance broker on the price and service differences between insurance companies)

- Dedicated phone and fax lines

- Full inventory

- Shelving and benches

Also, keep in mind that having a retail location requires additional licenses. Check your local city office to make sure that you comply with all the requirements. You may need a security alarm permit, a retailer license, and if you sell used computers, you may need a secondhand license.

2.1 Find a great location

Of course, if you want to open a retail store, you need to find a great retail location. When we opened our second store, the location was so wonderful that we were profitable the very first month! The following are some things to look for in a great retail location:

- **No immediate competition:** You may be able to do business against Best Buy's Geek Squad, but you still don't want to be across the street from a Best Buy or, worse yet, another small computer retailer.

- **Street visibility:** There are so many shopping centers that can't be seen from the street. While this is fine for businesses that are destinations (e.g., bowling alley, supermarket), for a small business such as a computer retailer, it would be nice to pull in customers who are driving by. After all, you are paying for retail space, so you may as well get the advertising benefits from it.

- **Parking:** Remember that customers will be bringing large desktops to your business. Don't choose a location that will make them walk a long way with a heavy computer — they simply won't do it. Instead, find a retail location that has parking spots available directly in front of the store. Furthermore, check the parking lot at various times of the day. The spots you want your customers to use should be open. If the shopping center is too busy then the center may not be a good place for a computer repair business.

- **Safety and security:** As a computer retailer, you will always have to consider the costs associated with security for your business. In general, the worse the location, the lower the rent, but your security costs and shrinkage (loss of product from theft) will be higher.

- **Compatible businesses:** One of the big things to look for in a location is what other businesses are around you. Obviously if the entire shopping center is vacant, your customer base will not be growing because of drive-by traffic. However, a shopping center with many different, growing businesses will actually generate sales for your store! One of our stores is directly next door to a Dunkin' Donuts which meant that hundreds of potential customers saw our store as soon as we opened!

- **Flexible signage rules:** Some shopping centers have very rigid rules about signs — basically they aren't allowed. Other places are flexible and allow businesses to advertise on the street, in the parking lot, and with banners. As a new business, it is always easier to launch your business in a business-friendly shopping center than in a more restrictive one.

2.2 Buying an existing store

Another way to expand your business is to buy an existing store that is already in operation. Small computer stores exist all over and you may find that some of the owners are willing to sell for the right price.

In general, the price of purchasing an existing business will be higher than the initial investment of starting a business on your own. When you start a business, you will pay for the cost of tangible assets such as inventory, equipment, plus about two times the "yearly net." This means that you not only pay for the assets, but you are giving the business owner two years of profit to buy his or her business. In return, you are receiving the business's existing customers, reputation, good will, and usually about one month of the owner's time to teach you the business.

Just make sure that you don't overpay for the business. The owners will try to show that their business is as profitable as possible. This means that many sellers will try to downplay expenses. In some cases, owners who are planning to sell will go as far as to drop advertising and other expenses a few months before they sell. Their hope is that sales will remain stagnant, but expenses will be low, thus increasing the appearance of profitability. Of course, when the new owners do buy the business, they may find declining sales, and reduced profitability.

In other cases, owners may want to sell because they know something you don't. Many people will say that they are selling to move out of town or to move on to a different investment, but that may not always be the truth. If a big-box store like Best Buy is moving in, a savvy business owner may decide it's time to move out!

The following are some of the things you can do to protect yourself:

- **Hire a lawyer:** Always get a lawyer for any large business transaction like this. The value of a lawyer's expertise will be worth his or her charge.

- **Hire a professional appraiser:** These individuals will know a business of this type and what the retail value is in your area. Like a home appraiser, these people will provide comparable sales for the business, and give you an idea of just what the business is really worth.

- **Review the financials:** Ask the business owner for all of his or her financial records for the last two years and have these reviewed by a professional accountant. Checking everything from tax returns to profit and loss statements will help you verify that the business hasn't changed dramatically (e.g., due to reduced advertising or a sudden drop in customer sales).

- **Negotiate everything:** The asking price of the business is just a starting point. Make sure that you negotiate for every penny. If there are new expenses that you need to pay, reduce your offer accordingly. If the owner dropped advertising, add that back into the expenses before you bid. Make sure that you are clear where your offer came from so that the owner realizes you are being fair and not just "lowballing" the bid.

If you are thinking about buying an existing store, www.BizBuySell.com is a great place to start investigating businesses. You can learn about what businesses are available and how much the owners are asking.

2.3 Buying into a franchise

Just because a company is offered as a franchise doesn't mean it will make money. As a matter of fact, there are plenty of franchise businesses that open and close each year. Before you buy a computer repair franchise, make sure to ask these important questions:

- What training does the franchise provide?

- What advertising and marketing does it do?

- What are the start-up costs and ongoing costs? (Most franchises take a percentage of every sale.)

- What has been the success or failure rate of the businesses in your area and in your state or province?

- Can you talk to other owners for references?

Today, there are many different franchise businesses and every owner has a direct impact. For instance, a few doors down from our first store was a franchised sandwich shop. The old owner ran it into the ground with food safety violations and poor customer service. The franchise was then purchased by a more professional owner who began growing the business immediately. So, before you get involved in a franchise, make sure you find out all you can about what makes a successful chain franchise.

3. You Can Make It Work!

Let's face it, none of us is perfect. When we first started in the computer repair business, my wife and I each had years of experience in IT and management. We purchased an existing store and even had the owners train us on the business. We had all the advantages we could and still we had problems with computers, trouble employees, and annoyed customers. Then the recession hit!

The key is to make sure that you learn from every failure and gain knowledge from every experience. Sure, things won't always go your way, but if you learn from the experience, you will find that things start getting better and not worse. Sometimes it is actually good to fail as fast as possible. What I mean by this is that you will oftentimes learn more by trying and failing than you will by preparing. While the lesson may seem expensive at first, when you realize what you learned from that experience and how much it can benefit you to go forward, you will realize that it was still a great opportunity.

When we first purchased our computer store, it was great. However, when the economy started failing, so did our store. To survive, we redesigned our business and recovered. For more information on low-cost (or free) ideas to increase sales, reduce your business expenses, and bring in new customers, read our first book: *19 Ways to Survive: Small-business strategies for a tough economy.*

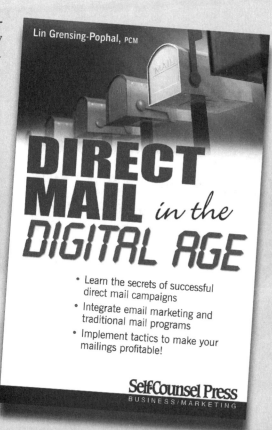

19 Ways to Survive: Small-Business Strategies for a Tough Economy

Lynn Spry and Philip Spry

ISBN: 978-1-55180-891-8

$19.95 USD/$21.95 CAD

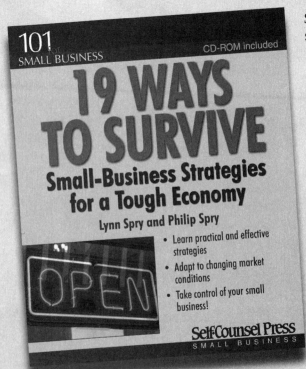

Strong economies come and go. Your business shouldn't have to!

You may have heard the statistic that nine of ten small businesses fail in the first five years of operation. Did you know that for those that make it to year six, an additional 90 percent fail over the next five years? This means approximately 99 percent of small businesses won't survive their first decade in operation.

By the authors of *Start & Run a Computer Repair Service*, the book *19 Ways to Survive* coaches small-business owners how not to fall victim to these statistics. The book presents practical solutions in easy-to-understand language.

Self-Counsel Press